America's Daughters

400 Years of American Women

Judith Head

Perspective Publishing
Los Angeles

Photo research by Diane Hamilton and Linda Goodman Pillsbury
Designed by Linda Goodman Pillsbury

Library of Congress Catalogue Card Number 99-2069
ISBN: 0-9622036-8-8

Published by Perspective Publishing, Inc.
2528 Sleepy Hollow Dr. #A, Glendale, CA 91206
800-330-5851; 818-502-1270; fax: 818-502-1272;
books@familyhelp.com or perspectivepub@loop.com
www.familyhelp.com

Additional copies of this book may be ordered by calling toll free 1-800-330-5851, or by sending $20.95
(16.95 + $4 shipping) to above address. CA residents add 8.25% ($1.40) sales tax. Discounts available for
quantity orders. Bookstores, please call LPC Group at 1-800-626-4330.

Library of Congress Cataloging-in-Publication Data

Head, Judith
    America's daughters : 400 years of American women / Judith Head. –
– 1st ed.
        p.   cm.
    Summary: A history of women in the United States from the
seventeenth century to modern times, discussing the roles they have
played in society and historical events and focusing on individuals
from Pocahontas to Sandra Day O'Connor.
    ISBN 0-9622036-8-8 (pbk.)
    1. Women—United States—History Juvenile literature. 2. Women—
United States—Social conditions Juvenile literature.   [1. Women—
History. 2. Women—Social conditions. 3. Women Biography.]
    I. Title
HQ1410.H4   1999
305.4'0973—dc21   99-2069
                                                              CIP

Printed in Hong Kong
First Edition

For my daughter, Austin Evelyn Head-Jones, and in
memory of my mother, Jo Benton "Ben-Joe" Flanagan Head

*The Becker sisters brand cattle on their ranch in the San Luis
Valley of Colorado in 1894. Moving to the frontier brought
new challenges. It also gave women the chance to break old
rules and start new traditions.*

*(Cover picture) Workers in a New Jersey shipyard report for
work on Labor Day, 1943. More than nineteen million women
held jobs during World War II, millions of them in trades that
had traditionally belonged to men.*

Contents

Hazel Campbell, on the left, sat for her photograph with her mother and sister in a Boston studio. (About 1919.)

Children play outside a one-room school in North Dakota in 1913. Margaret McKay, the twenty-year-old teacher, stands in the doorway. Sometimes children as young as four and as old as eighteen shared the same classroom.

The girls on this high school basketball team from Milton, North Dakota were lucky. Not many girls had the chance to play basketball in 1909. Even so, interest in sports for women was growing. Thirty-seven states had women's high school basketball teams by 1925. The sport's page of the New York Times even covered a few of the games.

For women on the frontier doing laundry was exhausting. Making soap from fat and ash, hauling water, gathering wood, and boiling and rinsing the wash often took a whole day. (About 1900.)

Introduction

Remarkable women are everywhere in America's past and present. They have won Nobel Prizes, served on the Supreme Court, led slaves to freedom, cooked in boarding houses, and tended the sick. Through effort and determination, they have overcome countless challenges to lead successful lives. Some became famous. Most did not.

Chien-Siung Wu was one of the few who did, but she faced many barriers along the way. Her father's sound advice guided her. "Ignore the obstacles," he told her when she was growing up in China. "Just put your head down and keep walking forward." Chien-Shiung Wu did just that. While still in China, she worked late into the night with borrowed books to teach herself math, physics, and chemistry so that she could study physics at a university.

Chien-Shiung Wu came to the United States to study physics in a graduate

school in 1934 at age twenty-two. When she finished she could not get a full-time job teaching in a university. No one would hire a woman as a physics professor. So she took part-time teaching and research jobs wherever she could find them.

Chien-Shiung Wu became a United States citizen in 1954. Two years later she tested a law of physics and found that subatomic particles did not perform the way the law predicted. *The New York Post* wrote that she was "powerful enough to do what armies can never accomplish: she helped destroy a law of nature." For her incredible experiment she won the Comstock Award given by the National Academy of Sciences only once every five years. She also became a professor at Columbia University and the president of the American Physical Society. Chien-Shiung Wu had the courage to keep going even though she faced setbacks.

Through the ages millions of American women have lived important lives. Some, like Chien-Shiung Wu, made great discoveries and became well-known. Other remarkable lives have passed almost unnoticed. Whether famous or unknown, America's women have left traditions of resolve, vision, and energy. This book looks at their amazing legacies.

As a young girl, Chien-Shiung Wu was determined to study physics. When she grew up, she disproved a law of physics.

1

1565 The Spanish establish St. Augustine in Florida, the first permanent European colony in North America.

1607 More than a hundred English colonists start a colony at Jamestown in Virginia. Pocahontas rescues Captain John Smith.

1620 Puritans establish a colony at Plymouth in Massachusetts.

1626 Dutch colonists buy Manhattan Island for $24 in trinkets and found New Amsterdam. The English conquer the city in 1664 and change the name to New York.

1634 A Catholic colony is started in Maryland.

1636 Exiles from Puritan Massachusetts found a colony in Rhode Island.

1600

1625

1600s

The Mason Children is a rare painting of children in early America. Like most portraits, this one contained many symbols. Joanna Mason's fan and ribbons show that the family was wealthy. Abigail's rose stands for childhood's innocence. (1670.)

1660 The British Parliament passes the Navigation Acts to keep American trade under British control.

1675-76 King Philip's War erupts in New England. Wars between settlers and Native Americans continue for more than 200 years.

1683 Delaware Indians sign a treaty with William Penn entitling him to buy land for a Quaker colony in Pennsylvania.

1698 The British Parliament passes the Woolens Act to prevent colonies from shipping wool to one another.

1692 Witchcraft hysteria breaks out in Salem, Massachusetts and other New England towns.

1650   **1675**   **1700**

A woman and man wind silk in this woodcut designed to attract settlers to early Virginia. Women, men, and children, too, had to work hard for the family to survive. (1650.)

Women's Work

Being born a girl or boy in the new colonies was the most important factor in a person's life, because it determined the way she or he was raised. Since most colonists came from Europe, they brought up their children according to European customs and laws. Girls learned to cook, garden, preserve food, milk cows, make butter, clean, spin, sew, care for younger children, and do a hundred other tasks. If their hands were not needed at home, older girls worked as maids in homes where help was needed. There they earned a little pocket money and polished their housekeeping skills. Girls also learned to read the Bible, but, unlike their brothers, most were taught little or no writing.

Husbands usually sold the goods the household produced, but women also traded. They bartered or sold cheese, butter, fruit pies, cloth, clothing, knits, and poultry. Mistress Hewlett of Ipswich, Massachusetts was one example. Her poultry business was so successful that she loaned money to her husband. Because a wife's earnings belonged to her husband by law, a friend asked Mr. Hewlett why he allowed his wife to control the money she earned. "I meddle not with the geese or turkeys for they are hers for she has been and is a good wife to me," he said.

Some women relied entirely on money they earned themselves. This was especially true for widows and unmarried women without family. Colonial governments would seldom grant women more than a few acres of land, so single women could rarely support themselves by farming. Many spun thread and yarn or wove cloth. Unmarried women who made their living by spinning were called "spinsters." These tasks took a lot of time and paid so little that many women who relied on them lived in poverty.

Some women taught young children in their homes in dame schools. These women earned only ten or twenty percent as much as male teachers. They were also forbidden to teach children over nine years old for fear that it would strain the women teachers' "weak brains."

Few women questioned the work they did, but some found ways to enter professions usually closed to women. Mrs. Jose Glover of Cambridge, Massachusetts owned the first printing press in the colonies. Margaret Brent and a few other women used money they had inherited to start businesses and careers. Most medical practitioners were women herbalists. Women were also barbers, carpenters, furniture makers, and metal workers. A few women had learned trades by working with their fathers, brothers, or husbands. With so few skilled people around, not everyone cared about a worker's gender as long as the job was done.

Whether or not women ran farms or businesses, they had total responsibility for the home. They worked from sun up to sun down and beyond, and they needed strength and courage for their hard, grueling lives.

Some children attended dame schools for a few hours each day. They learned spinning and other household skills, reading, and sometimes a little writing.

Women's Place

Almost all the young women in the colonies married, sometimes because marriage was the best way for them to make a living. Since many more men than women immigrated, every woman who wanted to marry found at least one suitor.

Religion was important to colonial women, and activities such as church, childbearing, illnesses, funerals, and helping one another with work kept women close. Childbearing was an important and dangerous time—and a social occasion. It was also one of the few events entirely controlled by women. Women friends, relatives, and the midwife gathered at the mother-to-be's home to help with the birth. They kept the father informed, but did not allow him into the birthing room. If the mother, baby, or both became ill or died during childbirth, the same women cared for the sick or prepared the departed for burial. Once the baby was born, it was a wife's duty to raise the child according to her husband's instructions.

Most men and women in seventeenth century Europe thought that women were weak in character and mind. Many colonists who settled the New World brought that belief with them. The governor of Massachusetts charged that too much study of serious issues had caused Ann Hopkins, the wife of Connecticut's governor, to lose her mind in 1645. He said that if she had

> attended to her household duties, and such things as belong to a woman, and had not . . . meddle[d] in such things as are proper for men, whose minds are stronger etc., she [would] have kept her witts and might have improved them . . . in the place God had set her.

Because women were considered weak, there were many things they were not allowed to do. In Puritan New England, they were forbidden to speak in both church and government. They could not vote or hold office. Women were "not to teach, not to hold authority over the man, but to be in silence." If a woman broke the rules and spoke up publicly, she might be accused of meddling and taken to court. Anne Hutchinson talked so boldly about her religious beliefs that leaders made her leave Massachusetts. She and her followers founded a new settlement in Rhode Island.

Women had few rights before the law. In New England only single women over twenty-one years old controlled their own property. The father of a woman under twenty-one or the husband of a married woman had the legal right to the woman's property and earnings. When Hannah Duston of Massachusetts killed and scalped nine Native Americans during King Philip's War, her husband collected the reward. Women in the southern colonies usually had a little more control. A wife, for example, had to agree to the sale of any land she had brought into a marriage, but she could not sell the property alone.

The law also required wives to obey their husbands. One Puritan pamphlet said that "woman was made . . . that man might rule over her." Women were sometimes fined or publicly whipped for disobeying too openly. But husbands owed their wives financial support, and men usually valued women, if only because running a farm, business, or home without them was difficult.

Although divorce was rare, it was more common in New England than in the middle and southern colonies, because the Puritans considered marriage a civil agreement rather than a religious commitment. When divorce did occur, the children belonged to the husband.

The strength women showed every day contradicted beliefs about their weakness. Women ran households requiring strenuous work and heavy responsibility. They also helped their husbands with businesses. When husbands were away, women added the upkeep of farms and shops to their own exhausting schedules. When men died, widows often kept farms and businesses going to support themselves and their children.

Women also acted independently even when it was not allowed. The women in Chebacco, Massachusetts had trouble walking to the nearest church several miles away while carrying their small children. With the men bogged down in debate, the women worked with people from several nearby villages to build a new church. They were charged in court and fined for "contempt of authority," but the new church remained standing.

The Quakers who began settling in New England after 1650 considered men and women equal before God, so Quaker women were allowed to speak and preach. When Quakers and Puritans came together, there were clashes. Quaker Dorothy Waugh of Boston, Massachusetts attempted to speak in a Puritan church one Sunday. She was accused of being a witch and sentenced to whipping. Mary Dyer, another Quaker, was eventually hanged for speaking out in Puritan churches.

Many Englishwomen who immigrated to North America wore hats and uncomfortable-looking neck ruffs that were popular in England at the time. (English print, 1640.)

Ojibwa women tie and cover the frames of their lodges or wigwams while the men sit nearby. The Ojibwa are also called the Chippewa. (Print, 1855.)

Native American Women

In many Native American cultures men waged war, hunted, and governed while women and girls did much of the other work. Women planted, cultivated, and harvested crops such as corn, beans, and squash. They made pottery and baskets, wove cloth, tanned hides for clothing and dwellings, made maple sugar, cared for children, dried and prepared food, and constructed housing. Early settlers described Native American women as always working, even though the men found time for leisure.

Like their immigrant neighbors, women in Native American tribes seldom had the same status or authority as men. Even so, they were sometimes very influential. Women managed the wealth in the Alaskan Tlingit tribe. The older women of the Seri in California controlled the property. Among the Zuni of the Southwest, men farmed while women owned the land. After the Spanish brought sheep into the Southwest, Navajo women owned most of the livestock. That meant women controlled most of the tribe's wealth. Also, Navajo family lines and inheritance were traced through women.

Native American women sometimes held high positions. Among the mid-western Shawnee, women were sometimes chiefs. Among the Iroquois of the Northeast they served as healers and spiritual leaders called shamans. Iroquois women also nominated chiefs and removed leaders who ruled badly.

Native American women were recognized for their bravery. The peaceful southwestern Hopi have a legend about a girl who was also a warrior. One day, while her mother was twisting one side of the girl's hair into a whorl, the two noticed enemies approaching. With one side of her hair coiled and the other side hanging loose, the girl grabbed her bow and arrows and saved the village.

Hopi girls grind corn. Most Hopi wore traditional dress, jewelry, and hair styles well into the twentieth century. (Photo, 1903.)

A Puritan family receives its meager daily ration during the first hard winter in the New World. The luckiest colonists lived in small log huts.

Anne Forrest & Anne Buras

Forrest & Buras—Born: date unknown, England   Died: date and place unknown

Even before colonists arrived from England, women from other European countries had come to North America. Francisca Hinestrosa might have been the first. She went with her husband to Florida and other parts of the South on Hernando de Soto's expedition in 1539. Twenty-six years later the Spanish founded St. Augustine in Florida. It became the first permanent European settlement in North America. Many of its colonists were women.

Anne Forrest and her thirteen-year-old maid Anne Buras came to Jamestown, Virginia, the first permanent English colony in the New World, in 1608. When they saw the year-old colony, they must have had the shock of their lives. Instead of the land of milk and honey advertised, the colony offered exhausting work, disease, drought, fires, Indian raids, and a famine so severe that it was called the "starving time."

More than ten years later in 1620 Puritans established a settlement at Plymouth in Massachusetts Bay. Its first year was as bad as Jamestown's. When their ship landed in December, the harsh New England winter greeted the colonists. Many people lived in tiny dugouts and sod houses that one settler described as "nasty, dirty, dank and cold." By winter's end fourteen of the eighteen women who had arrived on the *Mayflower* had died, but all eleven girls had survived.

Though conditions in the New World were not always as severe as those faced at Jamestown and Plymouth, the days were long and difficult. Women built fires, cooked, baked, made candles, spun yarn, wove cloth, sewed, knitted, made soap, hauled water, washed, milked, made cheese and butter, grew vegetables, preserved meats, vegetables, and fruit, raised poultry and pigs, bore, cared for, and taught children, tended the sick, and often worked in the fields. Women settlers led exhausting lives.

A few wives of the first Jamestown colonists arrived in 1608, a year after the men landed. The next year more than a hundred women came from England to marry the colony's men. A man paid 120 pounds of tobacco for a woman's passage. A woman worked in exchange for room and board until she decided which man to marry. (Print, 1876.)

Pocahontas pleads for Captain Smith's life. She was a hero in early America. (Engraving from John Smith's Generall Historie, 1624.)

Pocahontas

Born: about 1595, Powhatan Confederacy   Died: 1617, England

At age twelve or thirteen, Pocahontas rescued Captain John Smith, the leader of the Jamestown colony in Virginia. For years after, she served as a link between Native Americans and English colonists.

Smith was captured in 1607 near an important village in the Powhatan Confederacy. Powhatan, Pocahontas's father, was the Confederacy's leader. He was about to have Smith executed when Pocahontas convinced him to spare the Captain's life and have him escorted safely back to Jamestown. Smith later wrote that Pocahontas "hazarded the beating out of her owne braines" by stepping forward to protest. Smith called her "wit and spirit" extraordinary.

Several times in the years afterward, Smith appealed to Pocahontas to save the starving colony, and the young woman sent food. When the colonists captured some Native Americans in 1608, Pocahontas represented her father in the discussions to free them. Two years later she again saved the life of an Englishman threatened with execution by the Powhatan Confederacy.

Pocahontas was kidnapped in 1613 and taken to Jamestown. While there, she lived with an English family and adopted English dress. The next year she was baptized a Christian, took the name Rebecca, and married colonist John Rolfe.

The marriage assured peace between the colonists and the Powhatan Confederacy.

The couple sailed to England two years later. There King James and Queen Anne met Pocahontas and treated her like a princess. Pocahontas was not used to the wet, cold English weather or European diseases. She died just as she, her husband, and young son were about to return to America. Even though she was only twenty-two or twenty-three years old, her courage and intelligence had already saved many lives in colonial America.

A ship's captain from Jamestown lures Pocahontas on board an English ship and kidnaps her in 1613. (Engraving, 1618.)

Ætatis suæ 21. Aº. 1616.

Pocahontas visited England with her husband and son in 1616. Rebecca Rolfe was her married name. (Copy of a seventeenth century English painting.)

Anne Bradstreet

Born: 1612, England   Died: 1672, Massachusetts Bay

Anne Bradstreet was one of the best educated women in early America. No portrait of her has come down to us, but an artist painted her this way for a later biography. (Frontispiece, 1898.)

On the surface Anne Bradstreet was a model Puritan woman. She feared God, and loved and obeyed her husband. She ran an efficient household where she loved, cared for, and disciplined her children. According to her brother-in-law, she was admired "for her pious conversation, her courteous disposition, her exact diligence in her place." Even with all that, Anne Bradstreet was more than she appeared. She was also the first important American poet.

Anne Bradstreet came to the Massachusetts Bay Colony at age eighteen with her parents and husband. Even though she grew up in the Puritan church, she had

received an education available to few girls anywhere. In England her father had worked as a steward for the Earl of Lincoln at Tattershall Castle. Anne Bradstreet had read widely in the earl's library and had studied with tutors. After she settled in the New World she began to write poetry about love, family, history, nature, and other subjects.

She did not loudly challenge the seventeenth century idea that women were weak-minded and should keep silent, but her poetry showed that she did not always agree with the accepted view.

> I am obnoxious to each carping tongue
> Who says my hand a needle better fits,
> A poet's pen all scorn I should thus wrong,
> For such despite they cast on Female wits:
> If what I do prove well, it won't advance
> They'll say it's stol'n, or else it was by chance.

Anne Bradstreet wrote for herself, her family, and her friends. She never intended for her work to be made public. When her first book of poems was published anonymously and without her consent in 1650, she apologized because others would see the "ill-formed offspring of my feeble brain." Her humble response was just right for a Puritan woman, but one modern poet has called hers "the first good poems in America."

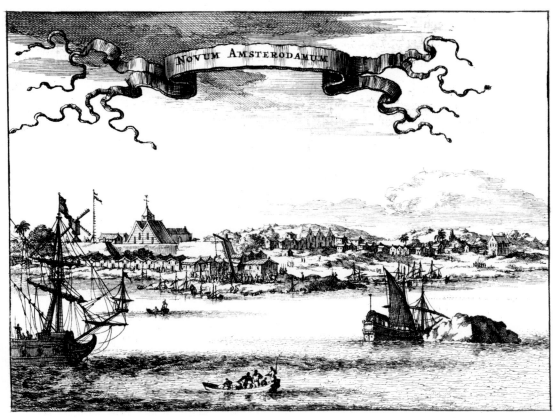

New Amsterdam, later renamed New York, as it looked when Margaret Hardenbrook Philipse lived there. (1671.)

Margaret Hardenbrook Philipse

Born: date unknown, Rhine Valley, Netherlands   Died: 1690, New York

Like many Dutch women, Margaret Hardenbrook Philipse was "bred to accounts, and affairs." That means she was active in business from an early age. She used her experience and good luck to become a wealthy businesswoman in North America.

Nineteen years after the English settled Jamestown, the Dutch founded a colony named New Amsterdam on the island of Manhattan. Like their Puritan neighbors, Dutch women in the New World could not participate in the political world. For generations, though, women in Holland had traded and conducted business. The Dutch women who settled in the New World did the same.

Margaret Hardenbrook probably arrived in New Amsterdam with a brother who had signed a contract as an indentured servant. By 1660 she was the North American agent for several Dutch merchants. She sold the goods they shipped from Holland and sent American products back to Holland for sale.

She married in 1660 and had a child. When her husband died the next year, she added his fur-trading business to her own. Even though she married again in 1662 and had four more children, Margaret Hardenbrook Philipse expanded her trading network and soon owned her own ship. She often sailed back and forth between Holland and New Amsterdam to supervise cargos and negotiate contracts. Sometimes one of her children traveled with her. She used her maiden name for business, even when she was married.

Margaret Hardenbrook Philipse made her fortune in shipping and trade. Seas, rivers, and the few canals that existed were the most important highways for moving goods and people in early America. (Sketch, about 1659.)

Millicent How & Other Indentured Servants

Born: date unknown, England   Died: date unknown, North America

Because life in the colonies was a struggle, few women were eager to settle there. Even so, thousands came from England, Ireland, Scotland, and other parts of Europe as indentured servants because they could not find jobs at home. Most indentured servants were eighteen to twenty-five years old and signed contracts promising to work between four and seven years. Some were kidnapped and carried onto ships or tricked into signing papers that bound them. Others, like Millicent How, signed papers of indenture voluntarily.

> Know all men that I Millicent How of London Spinster the day of the date hereof doe firmely by these pnts bind and oblige my selfe as a faithfull & obedient Sert in all things whatsoever to serve and dwell . . . in the plantation, or province of Carolina, according to the lawes & Customes and Orders for servts, wch are provided and settled in the said place. . . . Witness my hand and seale this pnt twentyeth day of September 1669.

Young women were usually shipped to the South where earlier colonists bought their contracts and took them to farms and plantations. They faced constant toil, often under brutal conditions. Their masters often forced them to

A seventeenth century cookbook illustration shows some cooking tasks. Indentured servant women often spent long hours in the kitchen and worked outside, too. (1684.)

labor in the fields, even if their contracts prohibited it. Many were starved, beaten, given meager clothing, and little or no bedding.

The indenture system was the main way of supplying workers for colonial farms and households during the first half of the seventeenth century, so its impact on the population was enormous. More than half the women who settled in the colonies before the American Revolution came as indentured servants. When their indenture ended, most of them married and had children.

Accounts about their lives are rare. Few indentured servants could write, and those who knew how had little time to write down their experiences. A ballad from the 1600s describes one woman's fate.

Five years served I, under Master Guy,
   In the land of Virginny, O,
Which made me for to know sorrow, grief and woe,
   When that I was weary, weary, weary, weary , O.

I have play'd my part both at Plow and Cart,
   In the land of Virginny, O,
Billets from the Wood upon my back they load,
   When that I was weary, weary , weary ,weary, O.

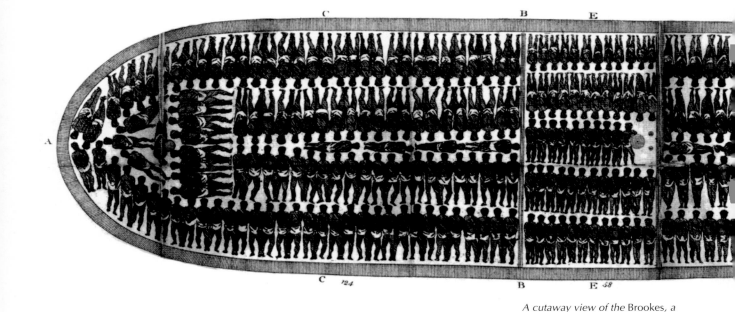

A cutaway view of the Brookes, a slave ship out of Liverpool, England, shows the way captives were stacked below decks. Men were stowed in the bow, boys in the center, and women in the stern. No one had enough room to move. Every phase of slavery was brutal. (Engraving, 1808.)

Isabella

Born: date unknown, Africa   Died: date unknown, Virginia

In 1619, a year before the *Mayflower* brought the Pilgrims to Massachusetts Bay, Isabella and nineteen other Africans arrived in Jamestown, Virginia. Baptized at sea and given a western name, Isabella married another African. Their son, William Tucker, is thought to have been the first African-American child born in the English colonies.

These first African Americans were indentured servants rather than slaves. When their contracts expired, they were freed, and the men were granted land. Like white indentured servants, they soon had families and small farms of their own. But by 1660 things had changed. Africans brought to the colonies were no longer freed. Slavery had begun in the colonies.

To find Africans for a growing market, slave traders bought prisoners of tribal wars, kidnapped people, and tore them from their families. They marched the captives to the coast, branded them, chained them by twos, and packed them into the holds of ships. Conditions were ghastly. According to one captain, "They had not so much room as a man in his coffin, either in length or breadth. It was impossible for them to turn or shift with any degree of ease." Disease and the horrible conditions killed so many people on the voyage that sharks commonly followed the slaves ships to feast on the bodies thrown overboard.

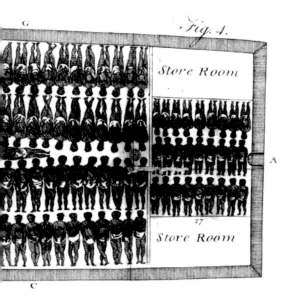

Fig. 4.

Store Room

Store Room

The voyage was called the "middle passage" because it was the middle leg of a trade route that ran from England to Africa, Africa to America, and back to England again. Most captives who survived the trip were sold to sugar plantations in South America or on islands in the Caribbean Sea. Others were shipped to the southern colonies, Boston, or Newport, Rhode Island. The Africans were traded for sugar, molasses, or tobacco that was usually sold in England. Then the ships were loaded with goods and set sail for Africa where their cargo was traded for more Africans.

Most captives remained slaves forever. They had no personal rights and no hope of better lives. For no other group that came to America was life so wretched.

*O my great massa in heaven.
Pity me and bless my Children!*

A slave trader leads a child away from its broken-hearted mother. More than two million Africans were shipped to North and South America as slaves during the 1600s. (Print, 1800s.)

Margaret Brent

Born: about 1601, England   Died: 1671, Virginia

Margaret Brent speaks in 1648 before the court of Maryland. She was probably the first woman in America to plead cases in court. (Magazine cover, 1926.)

Margaret Brent became one of the most influential women in the early colonies. When she arrived in Maryland from England with two brothers and a sister in 1638, she already had several advantages. First, she had the right to control her own property because she was grown and unmarried. Second, her parents were noble. Her mother was descended from an English king. Finally, she carried a letter from Lord Baltimore, who had established the colony of Maryland four years earlier, directing the governor to give each Brent a grant of land.

Margaret Brent was the first women to receive a land grant in Maryland. Baltimore, Maryland was named for the founder of the colony and became an important southern port and shipbuilding center. (Engraving , 1752.)

Because they were women, Margaret Brent and her sister received only small land holdings, but a brother deeded her more than a thousand acres from his grant to repay a debt. Margaret Brent was soon a powerful landowner, farmer, and businesswoman. She also became the first woman to argue cases in the Provincial Court of Maryland. She handled suits connected with her own businesses and pleaded cases for other people.

Lord Calvert, the governor of the Maryland colony, thought so highly of her abilities that he made her the executor of his will. That means he asked her to manage his property and affairs after he died. His death in May, 1647, came during a crisis. A two year rebellion of Protestants against Maryland's Catholic government had just ended. The soldiers who had silenced the rebels threatened to revolt if they did not receive food and their wages. To pay them, Margaret Brent sold pieces of land belonging to Lord Baltimore and to the late Lord Calvert. Lord Baltimore was angry when he learned that she had sold the land, but the Maryland Assembly defended her. "She rather desrved favour And thanks from your Honour for her so much Concurring to the publick safety."

Several months later Margaret Brent demanded for herself a vote in the Maryland Assembly. Since men who owned land had the right to vote in the assembly, she believed that she should, too. In fact she demanded two votes—one because she was a property owner and another because she was executor of the late Lord Calvert's lands. Despite the ability she had shown, she was denied even one vote, because she was a woman. Her response was to protest all future decisions made by the assembly.

Edmund Cheeseman's wife is tried for being a witch. A girl falling into fits during a trial was considered proof that the person charged with witchcraft was guilty.

Susanna Martin & Other Witches

Born: date and place unknown Died: 1692, Salem Village

Susanna Martin of Salem, Massachusetts was executed as a witch on July 19, 1692. She had been charged with causing girls to have fits. She was also accused of bewitching a man so that he could never own more than two cows. Susanna Martin was angry when one of her sons traded a cow to the man. The man testified in court that after he heard her "mutter," the cow

> broke all Ropes that were fastned unto her, and though she were Ty'd fast unto a Tree, yet she made her Escape, and gave them such futher Trouble, as they could ascribe to no cause but Witchcraft.

The account of her trial adds, "Note, This Woman was one of the most Impudent, Scurrilous, wicked creatures in the world."

Sixteen-year-old Mercy Short said a witch had cursed her. One day while working as a maid, she was sent to a prison on an errand. There a woman accused of witchcraft asked Mercy for tobacco. When the girl threw wood shavings on her instead of giving her the tobacco, the suspected witch responded with "ill words" which sent Mercy Short into fits. The woman was executed, but the girl's outbursts continued. During them she talked to the devil and accused him of trying to tempt her with fine clothes and a husband. Sometimes Mercy would frolic and dance. At other times she would criticize respectable people. Many people thought these actions showed that the devil possessed her.

One hundred forty-eight women were tried for practicing witchcraft in New England in 1692 and 1693. Often girls and young women between eleven and twenty years old charged middle aged women with bewitching them. Special courts heard the cases. The judges were prominent men from the church and community. Men testified against the so-called witches because it was improper for Puritan women and girls to speak in court except to answer questions. Sometimes the court assumed that those charged were guilty unless they could prove their innocence. Some women and a few men admitted that they were witches. A few probably believed that they were. Others confessed so that they would not be hanged.

Why did the witch craze occur? For some Puritans in early New England, the devil was everywhere. Consequently, witches, who were the devil's servants, might be everywhere, too. People seemed to abandon reason in hunting for them. The accused women were often outspoken, disagreeable, odd, or poor, while many of the girls who accused the older women led tightly controlled lives with bleak futures. For example, Native Americans had captured Mercy Short's family and killed everyone except Mercy. After the ghastly tragedy, the girl had no one to love and care for her.

The witch hunts show the influence young accusers might have in early New England's religious climate. They show even more clearly how difficult it was for women to defend themselves in a society where they had almost no legal voice and few rights.

The Wonders of the Invisible World:

Being an Account of the

TRYALS

O F

Several Witches,

Lately Executed in

NEW-ENGLAND:

And of several remarkable Curiosities therein Occurring.

Together with,

I. Observations upon the Nature, the Number, and the Operations of the Devils.
II. A short Narrative of a late outrage committed by a knot of Witches in *Swede-Land*, very much resembling, and so far explaining, that under which *New-England* has laboured.
III. Some Councels directing a due Improvement of the Terrible things lately done by the unusual and amazing Range of *Evil-Spirits* in *New-England.*
IV. A brief Discourse upon those *Temptations* which are the more ordinary Devices of Satan.

By *COTTON MATHER.*

Published by the Special Command of his EXCELLENCY the Govenour of the Province of the *Massachusetts-Bay* in *New-England.*

Printed first, at *Boston* in *New-England*; and Reprinted at *London*, for *John Dunton*, at the *Raven* in the *Poultry.* 1693.

Cotton Mather was an important Boston minister. He called witchcraft in Salem "as wonderful a piece of devilism as has been seen in the world." His sermons and writings fueled the craze. (Title page, 1693.)

Hundreds were accused of being witches in Salem Village. Nineteen were executed, one was tortured to death, and five died in jail. (Lithograph, 1892.)

1700 The population of North America is estimated at about one million. More than 10,000 Africans and about 350,000 Europeans and their descendants are among them.

1716 The first theater in the colonies opens in Williamsburg, Virginia.

1733 English debtors settle in Georgia.

1741 Slaves revolt in New York. As a result, 13 are hanged, 13 are burned to death, and 71 are deported.

1749 The Ohio Company receives a land grant of half a million acres. Colonists expand westward and clash with Native Americans and the French.

1700

1725

1700s

Women were important in the American Revolution. One of them, the wife of General Philip Schuyler, burned the family fields in upstate New York rather than let British troops have the grain.

1755-1763 The English fight the French and Indian War in North America and capture Canada.

1767 The English Parliament passes the Townshend Acts, slapping taxes on some imports and again angering colonists.

1766 England repeals the Stamp Act.

1765 The English Parliament passes the Stamp Act to help support the English army and government in America. The tax angers colonists.

1770 English troops kill five people during the Boston Massacre. The British Parliament cancels the Townshend Acts, except for the tax on tea.

1788 The United States Constitution goes into effect. The next year George Washington becomes the first president.

1775-1783 The American Revolution. The thirteen colonies wage a war for independence from England.

1790 3,929,000 people live in the United States, 95% of them in rural areas.

1791 The Bill of Rights is added to the Constitution, guaranteeing individual rights.

1750

1775

1800

Some children learned their abcs from alphabets with pictures. This one shows mostly street vendors. Five of the letters have pictures of women. (1700s.)

E e	Eels, live eels; large silver eels.
L l	Lobster buy my live lobster?
M m	Milk below maids, Milk from the cow.
N n	Newcastle Salmon, Delicate Salmon.
W w	Walnuts, rare cracking walnuts?

Women's Work

During the 1700s almost everything families needed was still produced at home, much of it by women. As in the century before, some girls went to dame schools for a few hours each day to learn reading, sewing, and needlework. Most, though, were taught domestic skills at home or sent to help friends and relatives.

Wherever they were, girls were busy. Fifteen-year-old Elizabeth Fuller of Princeton, New Jersey listed in her diary some of the work she did. One day she made pies, candles, cheese, minced meat for sausage, scrubbed floors, washed clothes, and attended to her main jobs, which were spinning and weaving.

Life was hard for everyone, but during this century there was some relief for wealthier women. They could buy dairy products, poultry, and homespun cloth made in the colonies. They could purchase tea, coffee, chocolate, and fine cloth

Most women worked at home or traded with their neighbors. Some also sold their wares in public markets, like this one in Philadelphia. (1798.)

shipped from England. The finer houses in towns were usually brick or clapboard and were more comfortable than the crude log or sod houses of the century before.

Most women carded wool, spun yarn and thread, and wove cloth, often for trade or sale. They continued to run dairies and raise and sell poultry. Women might exchange butter for cloth or trade baked goods for yarn. After 1750, a few merchants gathered women and girls into the first low-paying workshops. One Boston shop hired enough women to run 400 spinning wheels.

Chances for women to earn money were still usually related to domestic work, but there were many exceptions. Married women helped with family businesses and farms and managed them when their husbands were away or died. For twenty-three years after her husband's death, Ann Smith Franklin, Benjamin Franklin's sister-in-law, edited and printed the *Rhode Island Almanac.* Mary Musgrove, who had a Creek Indian mother and an English father, worked for the

governor of Georgia as an interpreter and advisor on Indian affairs. Women also operated boarding houses, inns, taverns, and small shops, and women were still midwives. Most colonial women, though, lived and worked at home, much as women had in the seventeenth century.

During the American Revolution, women worked even harder. With their husbands away, full responsibility for farms and businesses fell to them. Sometimes families lived in poverty because women became ill or could not juggle everything. Many women managed well. When Abigail Adams oversaw the family property during the Revolution, she increased her husband's wealth. Some women tackled jobs usually undertaken by men. A woman known only as Betsy the Blacksmith made cannon and guns during the war, and in South Carolina Mrs. Ramage operated a mule-powered cotton mill.

Women's successes did not bring them equality after the Revolution. Even so, the ability they showed, plus the popular ideas of liberty and democracy, gradually changed their position in society.

When he was grown, Lewis Miller made a sketchbook to show what it was like growing up in York, Pennsylvania. A few of the sketches show women he knew who cooked for hotels and taverns and owned them, too. "No Better And good Cooks Can be found no where," he wrote. (The York Hotels, Kept in 1800, drawn about 1850.)

Women's Place

"Remember the ladies," Abigail Adams wrote to her husband in 1776. On July 4, John Adams and the other members of the Continental Congress in Philadelphia had declared the American colonies independent of England. She wrote:

> In the new code of laws which I suppose it will be necessary for you to make, I desire you to remember the ladies. . . . Do not put such unlimited power into the hands of the husbands.

Abigail Adams had no formal schooling. Even so, she became one of the best-read women of her day, and the letters she wrote give us an insightful view into early America. (Portrait by Gilbert Stuart.)

Abigail Adams represented a new trend among women. Before the American Revolution few women questioned their place in society. During and after it, many objected both to restrictions placed on them and to being called inferior. The Constitution and laws of the new United States were disappointing to them. It left their legal position unchanged. After the Revolution a married woman's property still belonged to her husband. Women could not vote or hold office. Their presence in public activities was either prohibited or loudly denounced. Abigail Adams objected. "Emancipating all nations, you insist upon retaining absolute power over Wives."

Even so, the American Revolution brought some changes in women's lives. Many women, and men, too, insisted on more and better education for women. Before the Revolution only forty-five percent of America's women could read compared with ninety percent of the men. Women could not attend secondary schools or colleges. Yet they were still accused of being ignorant. Phyllis Mason, a student at one of the new academies for girls started after the Revolution, expressed the frustration that many women felt. "Men have denied us the means of knowledge, and then reproached us for the want of it," she said.

Girls' schools sprang up, and a few New England schools for boys started separate programs for girls. Because the schools charged tuition, girls from prosperous families benefitted the most. The Young Ladies Academy of Philadelphia, founded in 1787, was the first academy for girls in the new United States. Girls there studied reading, writing, grammar, geography, public speaking, and arithmetic. Ancient languages and literature, which were taught at most boys' schools, were not included in the curriculum.

Few people objected to the home as the center of a woman's world, but many now believed that girls needed knowledge to become good mothers and wives. People suddenly realized that women shaped the character of their children. As Sarah Pierce, founder of the Litchfield Academy for Girls in Litchfield, Connecticut, expressed it: the mother planted the "seed of vice or virtue" in children. Only an educated woman could raise the virtuous children that the new nation needed and also be "an agreeable companion for a sensible man." Writer and essayist Judith Sargent Murray and a few others went further. They favored more education so that women could support themselves.

A girl's diploma from the Litchfield Female Academy, founded in 1792. The requirements for a diploma were so high that only a few women who went to the school received them. Sarah Pierce started the academy when she was twenty-five to support herself and her family. Harriet Beecher Stowe and her sister, Catharine Beecher, were students there. (Silk diploma awarded to Lucretia Deming, 1819.)

The American Revolution changed ideas about marriage, too. Many women who had operated family businesses or farms during the Revolution began to think of marriage as a partnership. They did not believe that husbands should make all the decisions. Also, more women wanted to chose their husbands rather than leave the selection to their parents. A 1791 magazine article agreed. "It is she . . . that must spend her days with the man that she marries," it said.

By the end of the century, white women had expanded their place within marriages and families. As Judith Sargent Murray put it, "a conspicuous part on the grand Theatre of life" was now available to more and more women.

Another Lewis Miller sketch shows Mrs. Lottman cooking at her a tavern in 1799. Young Lewis eats her freshly cooked sweet potatoes. Fifty years later he remembered them as some of the finest he ever tasted. (Drawn about 1850.)

Slaves work on an indigo plantation in South Carolina. Eliza Pinckney introduced indigo into the South. (About 1773.)

Eliza Pinckney

Born: 1722, West Indies   Died: 1793, Philadelphia

Eliza Pinckney ran three plantations in the Carolinas at age seventeen. By the time she was nineteen, she had introduced a new cash crop into the region.

Young Eliza moved with her family from the West Indies to a plantation in South Carolina in 1736. Soon after, her father returned to Antigua where he served in the army. Because her mother was ill, Eliza ran the Carolina plantations. She managed finances, kept records, supervised planting and harvesting, and experimented with crops. She also carried on a lively exchange of letters with her father and others. She thrived on the independence and responsibility. She wrote to a family friend in 1740:

> Least you should imagine it too burthensom to a girl at my early time of life, give me leave to assure you, I think myself happy that I can be so useful to so good a father.

Eliza Pinckney experimented with several crops including indigo, a blue dye. After several failures she had a successful harvest and in one blow established her reputation as a fine planter and indigo as a new cash crop for the South.

At twenty-three, she married a wealthy planter, but continued to manage the lands she brought into her marriage. When her husband died thirteen years later, she ran his estates as well.

Three of the couple's four children lived to adulthood. Their two sons were generals in the Revolutionary War and later signed the Constitution of the United States. George Washington honored Eliza Pinckney with a visit near the end of her life and praised her as a model of American motherhood. When she died, President Washington asked to be a pall bearer at her funeral.

Eliza Pinckney wrote to her father for many years. In this letter she tells him about her upcoming marriage. Her feelings are typical of her time. (1744.)

Like many prosperous women and men in colonial America, Elizabeth Murray sat for her portrait. John Singleton Copley, the most famous portrait artist of the day, painted her, Mercy Otis Warren, Paul Revere, John Adams, and many other well-known people. (1769.)

Elizabeth Murray

Born: 1726, Scotland   Died: 1785, Boston

Through her own hard work and keen commercial sense, Elizabeth Murray became a prosperous Boston businesswoman. She immigrated to North Carolina from Scotland in 1739 at age thirteen to keep house for a brother who had bought a plantation there. Four years later the two returned to Scotland. When Elizabeth Murray again sailed for the New World with her brother and his new wife, she was determined to become independent. She brought with her enough cloth, thread, ribbon, and other dry goods to set up a shop.

While her brother and his wife continued south, she left the ship at Boston. She soon opened a shop selling fine cloth and thread and teaching fancy needlework. Six years later the inventory of her shop was worth seven hundred pounds, a lot of money in those days. She had become a successful businesswoman.

Elizabeth Murray traveled to England in 1754 to buy more goods for her shop and to take a course in bookkeeping. When she returned to Boston the next year, she married, and her property passed into the control of her husband. After her first husband died, Elizabeth Murray decided to marry again. This time she followed the lead of several other wealthy American women and asked her second husband-to-be to sign a financial contract. The contract gave her the right to control all the wealth she brought into the marriage. She also received another right usually denied wives. She could make a will and leave her property to whomever she wished. When she married for the third time eleven years later, she again used contracts to keep her property in her own hands.

Elizabeth Murray was ahead of her time in other ways, too. She thought that a girl could "improve her mind, time & fortune" through "usefull education." She also believed that girls should learn to be "useful members of society" and to support themselves.

Needlework was an expressive art form for many women. In this elaborate scene, Prudence Punderson of Preston, Connecticut tells about herself and her world, including birth, slavery, and adulthood. She also correctly predicts her own early death. She died in childbirth at age twenty-six, a year after she married. (About 1783.)

She helped several women start businesses. She gave gifts and loaned money to a Rhode Island woman so that she could start a school, and she helped two orphaned girls from Boston set up a shop. Although she had no children, she educated three nieces, including two daughters of the brother for whom she had kept house decades earlier.

Men and women rake hay. Many indentured women worked in the fields day after day. (Woodcut, 1806.)

Elizabeth Sprigs & Other Indentured Servants

Born: date and place unknown   Died: date and place unknown

Elizabeth Sprigs in 1756 wrote to her father in England about her miserable life as an indentured servant in Maryland. After working most of the day and night, her reward was to hear that she had not done half enough. She was

then tied up and whipp'd to that Degree that you'd not serve an Annimal. Scarce any thing but Indian Corn and Salt to eat and that even begrudged . . . Almost naked. No shoes nor stockings to wear . . . What rest we can get is to rap ourselves up in a Blanket and ly upon the Ground. This is the deplorable Conditions your poor Betty endures. And now I beg if you have any Bowels of Compassion left, show it by sending me some Relief. Clothing is the principal thing wanting.

In the eighteenth century the lives of indentured servants were as exhausting as ever. Many ran away to escape the backbreaking work on plantations and farms. Disease killed others, especially those living in the southern colonies. If a woman survived the ordeal and completed her service, she usually received a payment as required by law. It might be two dresses, a spinning wheel, other goods, or money.

A woman kneads bread beside the fireplace. A few lucky indentured women worked only in the house and yard. (Print, 1845.)

Marrying was less common for women whose contracts expired than during the 1600s. More men were moving west alone, so there were fewer around to marry. Instead, many women worked as household servants or started businesses based on domestic skills like spinning, weaving, sewing, or washing.

As the century advanced, fewer and fewer people came to the New World as indentured servants. By the time the American Revolution was over, black slavery had completely replaced the indenture system.

Tobacco was the most important crop in the early South. Indentured servants and slaves usually planted, tilled, harvested, and hung the plants to dry, then stripped and packed the leaves. (1750.)

Overseers made sure that slaves worked hard. (The Overseer Doing His Duty, watercolor by Benjamin Latrobe, 1798.)

Hannah & Other Slaves

Born: date and place unknown   Died: date and place unknown

Run away about the 15th of December last, a small yellow Negro wench named Hannah, about 35 years of age. . . . She has remarkable long hair, or wool, is much scarified under the throat from one ear to the other, and has many scars on her back, occasioned by whipping.

So read a sad notice in the *Virginia Gazette* on March 26, 1767. We will never know exactly what caused Hannah to seek her freedom at the moment she did, and we will never know her fate. But we can guess some of the horrors that made her run away. Using these and other facts, we can imagine the life of a woman locked in slavery during the 1700s.

Hannah might have been born after her mother was shipped to the southern colonies from Jamaica. She lived with her mother, father, brothers, and sisters in a small wooden shack on a plantation. While her mother and father worked in the fields every day, an old woman too weak for field work watched Hannah and the other children and told them stories. At age six Hannah started to work. She cared for younger children, carried water to the fields, or picked up rocks there. By the time she was ten Hannah worked in the fields from "can to can't," that is from the time there was enough light to see until darkness made outdoor work impossible.

Once a week Hannah's family was given three pounds of bacon and a basket of corn for each adult. Each child received half that amount. When Hannah's mother returned from work, she ground the corn into meal for bread and cooked the bacon while Hannah's father tended the planation's livestock.

Plantation owners encouraged births to increase the number of slaves they held, so Hannah might have had her first baby by age eighteen. By the time she was thirty-five she might have had twelve children. It is possible that when she ran away in 1767, her husband and all but her youngest child had been sold away from her.

Why did she receive so many beatings? Perhaps she slept through the bell that called the slaves to the fields. Maybe she protested the sale of a child, took fresh eggs for a sick relative, talked back to an owner or overseer, or tried to escape to freedom. Perhaps she had a brutal master. Regardless of the cause, she carried the scars of abuse all her life.

Negroes for Sale.

A Cargo of very fine ftout Men and Women, in good order and fit for immediate fervice, juft imported from the Windward Coaft of Africa, in the Ship Two Brothers.—
Conditions are one half Cafh or Produce, the other half payable the firft of January next, giving Bond and Security if required.
The Sale to be opened at 10 o'Clock each Day, in Mr. Bourdeaux's Yard, at No. 48, on the Bay.
May 19, 1784.   JOHN MITCHELL.

Thirty Seafoned Negroes

To be Sold for Credit, at Private Sale.

AMONGST which is a Carpenter, none of whom are known to be difhoneft.
Alfo, to be fold for Cafh, a regular bred young Negroe Man-Cook, born in this Country, who ferved feveral Years under an exceeding good French Cook abroad, and his Wife a middle aged Wather-Woman, (both very honeft) and their two Children. Likewife, a young Man a Carpenter.
For Terms apply to the Printer.

Humans were advertized and sold as casually as cattle or furniture. (Advertisement, 1784.)

*The driver's whip unfolds its torturing coil.
"She only fulks—go lash her to her toil."*

A woman comforts a child. Many overseers used whips to keep slaves working. (Print, early 1800s.)

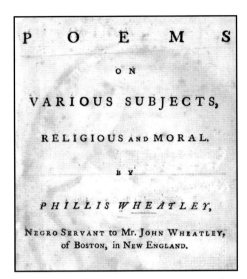

Phillis Wheatley was the first well-known African-American poet. Her book of poems was published in 1773. (Title page and frontispiece, 1773.)

Phillis Wheatley

Born: about 1753, Africa   Died: 1784, Boston

> I, young in life, by seeming cruel fate
> Was snatch'd from Afric's fancy'd happy seat:
> What pangs excruciating must molest,
> What sorrows labour in my parent's breast?

Phillis Wheatley had an international reputation as a poet before she was twenty-one. She was captured in Africa as a child and purchased from a slave ship in Boston by John Wheatley. She was so gracious and intelligent that Mr. and Mrs. Wheatley raised her as though she were their own child. The Wheatley twins, who were ten years older than Phillis, soon taught her to read, speak, and write English. By the time she was in her early teens, she was writing poetry. Her intelligence and poise won her invitations to the homes of Boston's white elite.

Phillis Wheatley sailed to England in 1773. The nobility entertained her, and her book, *Poems on Various Subjects, Religious and Moral,* was printed. Only five weeks after Phillis Wheatley reached England, she was on her way home, because Mrs. Wheatley had fallen ill. Mrs. Wheatley died the next year, and John Wheatley died soon after. With their parents' deaths, the Wheatley children abandoned Phillis and so did the public.

When Phillis Wheatley published a poem celebrating General George Washington in 1776, he invited her to visit him in Cambridge, Massachusetts and her career had a brief revival. Soon, though, she was thrust into surroundings more typical for an African-American woman in the northern United States during that time.

She married in 1778 and bore three children. Two of them soon died. Because Phillis Wheatley was an African American and a woman, the best job she could find was cleaning in a rundown boarding house. Too delicate for such hard physical labor, she became ill. Phillis Wheatley and her third child died on the same day. She was about thirty years old.

Like most poetry of that time, Phillis Wheatley's work usually focused on religion or morality. She wrote only a few poems about her life as an African-American woman. Her fine abilities, though, disproved the widespread opinion that African Americans were neither intelligent nor capable of learning.

Phillis Wheatley was bought from a slave ship in Boston, a city famous for freedom. The State House stands at the center of this illustration. (1791.)

Mercy Otis Warren

Born: 1728, Barnstable, MA   Died: 1814, Plymouth, MA

Mercy Otis Warren received an education available to few girls in the English colonies, and it helped her become a well-known writer. As a girl she gained her father's permission to sit in on her brothers' lessons and read the books in her uncle's library. When one brother stopped going to the lessons and the other left for college, Mercy kept studying.

Mercy Otis Warren was a Puritan woman brought up with a strong sense of duty, and for years she followed the traditional path expected of her. She married at twenty-six and bore five sons. Even with her busy life, she continued to read and in 1759 began writing poetry for pleasure. She found that she could finish her household duties with the help of a faithful servant and still have time for "the book and the pen."

Mercy Otis Warren used her pen to fight for the American Revolution. (Painting by John Singleton Copley, about 1763.)

The American colonies became more and more discontent with English rule after 1760, and Mercy's family was in the thick of things. A brother led the attack in Boston against the Stamp Act. John and Abigail Adams and other

This picture told young women that they should be quiet, industrious, and dutiful. Mercy Otis Warren was industrious and dutiful, but she wrote boldly and let people know what she thought. (Keep within the Compass, 1785-1805.)

patriots visited the Warrens in Plymouth, Massachusetts to plan resistance against the British. Mercy Otis Warren's husband, James, started the Committees of Correspondence to share information about the British. Some historians believe that his idea for the Committees came from the brisk exchange of letters between his wife and Abigail Adams.

John Adams urged Mercy Otis Warren to use her writing talents for the patriotic cause. At age forty-five, duty and her intelligence finally came together, and she published a play making fun of the royal governor of Massachusetts. After that she wrote other plays and poems.

When the Revolution was over, she continued writing about politics. She published a pamphlet opposing the United States Constitution because it had no Bill of Rights and gave so much power to the central government. She published a collection of poems, plays, and other writings at age sixty-two and a three volume history of the American Revolution at age seventy-seven.

Mercy Otis Warren sometimes felt discontent. On the one hand, she occasionally wished she were a man so that she could break the "narrow bounds" of her life. On the other, she did not think she lived up to the model of "gentleness, charity, and piety that adorned the female of earlier times." At a time when most women were seen rather than heard, her accomplishments were remarkable.

Revolutionary Women

The well-known British politician Edmund Burke spoke in 1779 about the role that America's women played during the Revolution:

> If they had not been rebels, I could have been lavish in praising women, who, reduced . . . to the most horrid situations of distress and poverty, had generosity and public spirit to strip the blankets, in the freezing season, from themselves and their infants, to send to the camp, and preserve that army which had gone out to fight for their liberty. . . . A three years war had not terrified them, distressed as they are, from their great purpose.

Like many other Revolutionary women, Mrs. Richard Wallace ran the family farm in Vermont while her husband fought. (National Life Insurance advertisement, 1943.)

During and after the American Revolution it was obvious to everyone that women were important in winning the war. Even before the fighting broke out women led the boycott of British goods. Instead of purchasing cloth from England, women wove or bought "homespun," just as they had during the first one hundred and fifty years in the colonies. Women also challenged British sympathizers. When a man denounced the Revolution at a mass meeting of the Daughters of Liberty, the women stripped off his coat and shirt and covered him with molasses and flower petals.

During the war women's organizations raised money and made clothes for the troops. The Ladies Association of Philadelphia collected money for supplies and sewed clothing. One British sympathizer said that the group campaigned so hard for money that "people were obliged to give them something to get rid of them."

Women were also spies. Deborah Champion disguised herself as an old woman and went on a special mission for George Washington. Sybil Luddington rode out to announce that the British were coming. Women broke new ground during the Revolution by writing and talking about politics. Some like Sarah Jay apologized in their letters for "dipping into politicks," because it was not a women's rightful territory. Others, like Mercy Otis Warren, spoke boldly.

The contributions of women to the American Revolution were widely praised during the 1770s and 1780s, but a century later Abigail Adams's grandson wrote:

> The heroism of the females of the American revolution has gone from memory with the generation that witnessed it, and nothing, absolutely nothing, remains upon the ear of the young of the present day.

Today we know enough about the past to once again salute the women.

Nancy Hart was a hero of the American Revolution. After Tories invaded her Georgia home and made her cook dinner for them, she killed one, wounded another, and held the others at gunpoint until help came. She and her rescuers then hanged the rest.

Deborah Sampson was so determined to fight the British that she dressed as a man and joined the Continental Army. After the war she toured the northeastern states, giving talks about her experience as a soldier. (1797.)

Deborah Sampson & Other Soldiers

Born: 1760, Plympton, MA   Died: 1827, Sharon, MA

At age twenty Deborah Sampson disguised herself as a man and joined the army to fight for the American Revolution. Strong and tall, she had been indentured as a domestic servant in Massachusetts at age ten. A decade later she walked more than seventy miles to enlist in the army.

Deborah Sampson kept her gender a secret from the army for a year and a half. Someone in her home town must have heard about her deception, though, because her church excommunicated her for "dressing in men's clothes, and enlisting as a Soldier in the Army." She fought in several clashes and was wounded, but still no one found out that she was a woman. Finally she was hospitalized with a fever and her secret was discovered. After she was discharged from the army, her story spread and a book was published about her. Despite her fame, she remained poor. In 1804 Paul Revere helped her get a soldier's pension of $4 a month.

Most women who supported the army during the American Revolution did not use disguises or become soldiers. Like other military forces of the day, the Continental Army did not have cooks, launderers, or nurses. Women, many of them soldiers' wives, traveled with the army and did that work.

A few of these women also fought in battles. Mary Ludwig Hays McCauley, or "Molly Pitcher" was the most famous. She earned her nickname when she carried

water from a spring to soldiers during the Battle of Monmouth in June, 1778. When her husband collapsed from the heat, she took his place loading a cannon until the long battle ended. Another Molly, Margaret Cochran Corbin, replaced her husband when he was seriously wounded at the Battle of Harlem Heights in 1776. She was also wounded and eventually lost the use of an arm. She was reburied in West Point Military Cemetery more than a century after she died as a tribute to her military service.

Because of her heroism during the Battle of Monmouth, Molly Pitcher was given a pension of $40 a year by the Pennsylvania legislature in 1822.

Martha Ballard

Born: 1735, Oxford, MA   Died: 1812, Augusta, ME

Martha Ballard's skilled hands delivered 814 babies in Hallowell, Maine between 1785 and 1812. Traveling through snow, rain, mud, and across a frozen river, she sometimes went from patient to patient for several days before returning home.

A midwife had to care for her home and garden as well as her business. Her life was easier if she had daughters or servants to help. (1780.)

Martha Ballard lived much like other eighteenth and nineteenth century midwives. She married and bore nine children. Six of them lived to adulthood. As a wife and a midwife, she had to juggle work at home with delivering babies and caring for the sick.

Being a midwife was strenuous. At two o'clock on the morning of December 6, 1793, Martha Ballard traveled by sleigh to a woman in labor. After the baby was born at noon, she moved on to another house and delivered a baby there at half-past nine that evening. At four o'clock the next afternoon she finally crossed the frozen Kennebec River to return home. She wrote that she spent a restless night because of "fatigue and wet feet."

Her diary entry for November 18, 1793, shows what a social event a birth could be.

> At Capt Meloys. His lady in labour. Her women calld (it was a sever storm of rain Cleard of with snow). My patient deliverd at 8 hour 5 minute Evening of a fine daughter. Her attendants Mrss Cleark, Dutton, Sewall, & myself. We had an Elligant supper and I tarried all night.

In the margin next to the entry, she marked XX to show she had received her fee, which was usually six shillings.

Using herbs from her own garden, Martha Ballard also tended the sick. She helped two families during a canker rash, or scarlet fever, epidemic on August 7, 1787.

Then she traveled

to Joseph Fosters to see her sick
Children. Find Saray & Daniel very ill.
Came home went to the field & got
some Cold water root. Then Calld to Mr
Kenydays to see Polly. Very ill with the
Canker. Gave her some of the root. I
gargled her throat which gave her great
Ease.

Martha Ballard lived in an age when
men seldom helped with children, the
household, or the garden. In the diary
entry above, for example, she assigned
the property to Joseph Foster, but in her
mind the children belonged to the
mother.

Martha Ballard's busiest years as a
midwife came when her daughters were
old enough to do the work at home.
When they married, all the work again
fell to her. She wrote on May 15, 1809:

In Martha Ballard's day, far
more midwives than male
doctors helped with
childbirth. As time passed,
doctors gradually replaced
midwives. This cartoon
mocks their growing presence
at births and their frightening
tools. (A Man-Mid-wife or a
newly discovered
animal, 1793.)

I have dug ground west of the hous. Planted squash, Cucumbers, musk and water
mellon East side house. Began and finisht a Large wash after 3 O Clock. Feel
fatagued.

No wonder she was tired. She was seventy-three years old. A month before
she died at seventy-seven, she was still delivering babies.

Martha Ballard's life sounds astonishing, but she probably lived much like other
midwives in the young country. Few left records, because even when women
knew how to write, they seldom had the time.

Heavy rains and
floods sometimes
destroyed the
bridges over the
Kennebec River in
Maine. Midwife
Martha Ballard
crossed the
flooded waters in a
canoe and walked
across the ice.
Once she fell waist
deep into ice-filled
waters, but made it
across in time to
deliver a baby.
(Engraving, 1823.)

1801 5.3 million people live in the United States.

1803 The Louisiana Purchase doubles the size of the new nation.

1814 The first power loom in the United states ushers in the Industrial Revolution.

1830 and after Photography is developed and becomes more and more popular as the century progresses.

1831 and after Abolitionists work to end slavery.

1844 The idea of Manifest Destiny gains popularity. It holds that all the land between the Atlantic and Pacific Oceans is destined to become part of the United States.

1848 The first women's rights convention is held at Seneca Falls, New York.

1800

1825

1800s

The Chrisman sisters stand in front of their sod house on the Nebraska prairie in 1886. Each young woman had filed a claim for 160 acres.

1861-1865 The Civil War ends slavery and restores the Union.

1861 and after Industry and big business boom in the North. The Civil War shatters the South.

1869 The Transcontinental Railroad speeds settlement of the West.

1890 The massacre of Sioux at Wounded Knee, North Dakota ends two and a half centuries of Native American resistance to white expansion across North America.

1850 and after The sewing machine revolutionizes the garment industry and sewing at home.

1873 and after The first commercial typewriters open new jobs for women.

1881 53 million people live in the United States. More than five million immigrants arrive during the next ten years.

1850

1875

1900

51

More than half the workers in tobacco factories were women by the end of the century. Children as young as five or six worked there, too. Here a young girl carries boxes while women roll cigarettes. Massachusetts passed one of the country's first child labor laws in 1842. It said that children younger than twelve years old could not work in a factory more than ten hours a day. (1887.)

Women's Work

During the nineteenth century the growth of industry and cities created more work for girls and women outside the home than ever before. Thousands moved from farms into cities to earn wages in water-powered textile mills. Others found work as servants in homes. Still others made shoes in factories, tended vending carts in markets, scrubbed clothes in laundries, and clerked in shops. Near the end of the century, women also pounded typewriters, ran sewing machines, and collected fares on streetcars. Throughout the 1800s thousands of young women became teachers, often with little education themselves.

The new textile industry offered some of the highest paying jobs available to women. They might earn as much in a day as a domestic worker brought home in a week. At the giant mill complex in Lowell, Massachusetts, women's wages ranged from thirty-five to fifty cents for a fourteen hour workday in a six day workweek.

Women who sewed the cloth produced in Lowell earned much less. Most averaged about twenty-five cents a day, but many earned as little as seventeen cents for twelve hours of work. Even with such low wages some employers tried to avoid paying them.

Women who worked as servants had long, hard days, but they earned about the same amount of money each week as school teachers.

Middle and upper class women often hired people to work in their homes, so more women worked in domestic service than at any other job. These were often young women and girls who had recently immigrated to the United States. They worked between eleven and fifteen hours a day. Women domestic servants earned fifty cents for a six day week in 1815. The average male laborer earned $1.25 a day.

Women workers were usually young. If they married or became pregnant, many left work or were forced to quit. Widows and wives who needed an income often worked for low wages at whatever jobs they could find.

Most women did not work outside the home, but they labored quite hard inside it. Almost all the work within the home was left to them and their daughters: cooking, washing, sewing, beating rugs, sweeping, scrubbing, dusting, making and changing beds, cultivating gardens, shopping, raising children, caring for the sick, and more. Most women who stayed home cooked large meals every day and baked twice a week. They boiled and rinsed the wash one day each week and ironed the next.

In the summer they canned. On a July day in 1870, one woman wrote in her diary: "I have a stiff neck and shoulder but have made ten pounds of strawberry jam." The next day she prepared ten quarts of black raspberry jam, and she canned five quarts of berries the day after. Four days later she canned three and a half quarts of raspberries and currants and the next day ten quarts of raspberries, two quarts of currant juice, two jars of cherries, and she also made pickles. It is no wonder that one daughter wrote: "Mama, with all her noble and ennobling ambitions, is a slave to the kitchen." Most women did not have the money to hire anyone to help. For them maintaining a home was exhausting.

Women's Place

A woman's place during the nineteenth century was standing in front of looms in a mill, walking beside a wagon across the prairie, teaching in a school, sewing in a sweatshop, or kneading bread in a kitchen. No matter where they were, women were now considered the heart of the family and the center of the home. Their presence within it was important and honored. Even in the United States, the century was often called the "Victorian Age" in honor of Queen Victoria of England. The queen was a capable and powerful monarch, but her private life centered around her family.

Most women were too busy and tired to live up to this romantic image of motherhood and womanhood. (Lithograph by N. Currier, 1846.)

Many people now believed that women were morally superior to men. Wives and mothers were expected to create homes that were havens from an industrialized world filled with greed and aggression. Shaping children into capable citizens became their responsibility. The Victorian view of women placed huge responsibilities on them, but it also gave them a purpose. It was their duty to guard the country's morals and pass them on to their children. This image of womanhood crossed the country from east to west, and many women tried to live up to it.

Magazines like Sarah Hale's *Ladies Magazine* and *Godey's Ladies Book* as well as books and articles by Catharine Beecher set the standard. Catharine Beecher, a sister of novelist Harriet Beecher Stowe, put women on a pedestal. She told women that their place was at home and in schools. She said that because of them families would flourish like well-tended gardens.

In her bestselling book, *A Treatise on Domestic Economy*, which sold for fifty cents in 1841, Catharine Beecher told women how to run efficient homes and raise fine children. Some of her practical advice sounds modern. Stay fit through calisthenics, she recommended, and avoid unhealthy fashions such as tightly laced corsets. Overlook a child's mistakes and teach through "rewards more than penalties."

But Catharine Beecher's noble mission had drawbacks. It restricted women to homes and schools. She said that a woman should not step into the broader world of politics or business where she would become a "combatant."

Many women considered this picture of Victorian womanhood too narrow and isolating. They believed that women had the right to a life outside the home. Harriet Beecher Stowe was one of them. She shrugged off her sister's advice and campaigned against slavery.

Other women needed work outside the home to earn money for themselves and their families. Women struggling to grow food on the prairie or working fifteen hours a day as domestic servants seldom had time to run a perfect home.

Women who considered the home too limiting pressed for change. Some worked through unions and factories for better pay and more jobs for women. Others helped the poor. Many middle class women in towns and cities opposed slavery through abolitionist organizations and crusaded against alcohol in temperance unions. They campaigned for the right to vote and to control their own property. Women were so effective at pushing for property rights that by 1900 married women had gained them in most states.

Many of these active women were criticized for speaking in public. They were told to go home where they belonged. But they didn't, and their successes gave them the confidence to work harder and step further onto the political stage.

Well-known lawyers in New York City tried to help seamstresses collect unpaid wages through the Working Women's Protective Union. (1874.)

Young women tended textile looms under the watchful eyes of male supervisors. (1836.)

Hannah Borden & Other Mill Girls

Born: date and place unknown   Died: date and place unknown

The lives of Hannah Borden and many other farm girls changed dramatically in the early nineteenth century when water-powered textile mills were built in New England. Young women left family farms to work in mills where they spun thread or wove wool and cotton on looms. Domestic skills learned at home suddenly earned good wages.

Their busy lives were filled with work. The factory bell awakened Hannah and the other girls at four in the morning at their boarding house in Fall River, Massachusetts. By five they were in the factory. Girls who arrived late found the front gate locked and either lost their wages for the day or paid a fine to have the gate opened.

Hannah and the others rushed back to their boarding houses at seven-thirty for breakfast and at noon for dinner. Thirty minutes later they were in the mill again.

There they stayed until seven-thirty in the evening. By the time they returned to their boarding houses, many were too tired to eat.

All day the young women stood at their looms. Some glanced at a favorite poem they had tacked nearby. All year the windows were sealed to lock in the moisture that kept the threads from breaking. During the summer the workers suffered from heat and humidity. During the dark "lighting season" of fall and winter, they breathed the unhealthy smoke from oil lamps.

After work or on Sunday afternoons those who were not exhausted could enjoy a rich cultural life. They might attend lectures, concerts, or discussion groups. They could read or write stories and poems for the factory newspaper. At ten o'clock the house matron locked the front door of the boarding house, and the lamps were turned out.

Why did they come? Why did they endure such a hard life? As hard as mill work was, it was easier than work on the farm. And they were paid for it. Girls who stayed on the family farm worked hard and rarely earned any money. Even mill girls who sent part of their wages back home or to a brother for his college tuition had something left for themselves.

Not all workers were content. Some banded together in 1846 and started the Female Labor Reform Association. Even though they were ridiculed for speaking out, they campaigned for a ten hour work day and better working conditions. "Try Again" was their slogan. It was a good choice, because more than half a century passed before they reached their goals.

Six days a week people surged toward the mills in time for the morning bell. Later in the century, immigrant girls and their families gradually replaced young farm women in the textile mills. (Engraving from a drawing by Winslow Homer, 1868.)

Families searching for homesteads moved west over beautiful and rugged land.
(A Journey Through the Navajo Country. The Halt, *photo by Ben Wittick, about 1890.)*

Sarah Bryan & Other Pioneers

Born: date and place unknown   Died: date and place unknown

During the nineteenth century thousands of women crossed the eastern mountains and the Mississippi River to the Great Plains and beyond. Some moved west willingly. Others had no choice. On foot, in wagons pulled by oxen, and on horseback, they traveled with parents, husbands, children, or alone. Even though almost all of them went west to claim new homesteads and build better lives, their journeys were almost always difficult.

Along the way they lived on beans, bacon, and, if they were lucky, bread and preserved fruit. Since wood was scarce on the prairie, many women collected buffalo dung, called "buffalo chips," for camp fires. Some even burned buffalo chips inside their wagons to keep away swarming mosquitoes. Whenever their wagons stopped for a day, the women made soap and boiled their wash.

When families arrived, they built primitive homes, much like those American settlers had lived in during the 1600s. Many put up sod huts. Others raised log cabins. Some lived in wagons or tents until they had the chance to build anything at all.

Sarah Bryan moved west with her husband, five children, and two yoke of oxen in 1823. They traveled through thick forests to the shores of Lake Huron. It was a hard journey, with "my husband cutting the road before us with an axe." The Bryans were luckier than most settlers. When they reached Lake Huron, they found an empty log cabin and lived in it until their own was finished.

Little more than a month after they moved into their own cabin, a sixth child was born. Sarah Bryan's husband set out across the woods to look for work soon after the birth. While he was gone, Sarah Bryan and the children nearly starved on their meager store of potatoes. "The neighbors were nearly as destitute and had nothing to lend," she said. Her husband's return made things easier, but "our sufferings for five or six years after this were even greater, if possible, than before." Like many pioneers the Bryans did not stay put. They and their children, now numbering eight, headed west again in 1835 and started their struggle anew.

Many women who moved west tried to uphold eastern standards. They brought pianos and decorated their sod houses with lace curtains. Others staked claims and started ranches. A few western women led unusual lives. California's famous stagecoach driver Charlie Parkhurst was a woman, but no one knew it until she died. Mary Fields, a former slave, protected the Ursuline nuns in Ohio and Montana. After that she delivered the mail and earned the nickname "Stagecoach." She didn't

Most settlers felt alone and surrounded by danger. (1826.)

miss a day of work until she was eighty years old. Narcissa Prentiss Whitman moved from New York state to the rugged Northwest in 1836 to teach Native Americans and convert them to Christianity. She was eventually killed in an Indian raid. Mary Jane Caples baked and sold pies to prospectors during the California Gold Rush and earned more than a hundred dollars a day. For most women, moving west was the adventure of a lifetime.

Emma Willard spent more than half a century as a teacher and educator. The school she founded trained many girls who became teachers, some in the South and newly settled West. (About 1840.)

Emma Willard

Born: 1787, Berlin, CT   Died: 1870, Troy, NY

The American Revolution promoted the view that both girls and boys needed an education to become good citizens. More education for girls required more teachers, and women filled the gap. Because women's salaries were much lower than men's, many schools welcomed them.

Emma Willard became a teacher as a young woman, but she went further. She founded the first school for women that offered the same demanding subjects as schools for men.

Emma Willard was born into a Connecticut farm family and had sixteen brothers and sisters. Her upbringing was traditional in many ways. When the sheep were sheared, the best wool went into clothing for her father and brothers. The leftover wool clothed her mother and the

The Troy Female Seminary in Troy, New York looked quite different than today's Emma Willard School. (1820s.)

girls. Even though boys were more important than girls in the household, Emma's father believed in education for girls. He sent Emma to school and introduced her to good books.

Young Emma was a bright student. At thirteen she taught herself geometry. At fifteen she enrolled in the Berlin Academy in Berlin, New Hampshire. Two years later she landed a job teaching the town's children. After a few years she became a teacher at the academy for girls in Middlebury, Vermont.

Emma Willard married in 1809 and stopped teaching, but when money ran short five years later, she opened a school for girls in her home. She was not satisfied with the courses offered in most girls' schools, so she taught some of the same subjects that young men studied.

This is a primary or lower school class in Gurley Hall at the Seminary. (About 1895.)

Emma Willard moved to Troy, New York in 1820. The next year she started the Troy Female Seminary, a private school for girls. The academy was the first school for girls that offered the sciences, mathematics, history, and modern and ancient languages.

Young women were eager for the serious education she offered. Within ten years the school had three hundred pupils. Fifteen years after her death, the institution was renamed the Emma Willard School to honor her. It is still an excellent girls' school today.

Maria Mitchell's fascination with the stars began when she was young. (Portrait by Hermoine Dassel, 1851.)

Maria Mitchell

Born: 1818, Nantucket Island, MA
Died: 1889, Lynn, MA

Maria Mitchell was so good at searching the stars with a telescope that she discovered a comet. Not only was the comet named for her, but her discovery brought her international fame and a gold medal from the king of Denmark.

Maria Mitchell believed in science education for women. Here she and her students at Vassar set up equipment for nighttime observations. (1878.)

Maria Mitchell's father was a self-taught astronomer. As a child she helped him watch the stars from Nantucket Island off the coast of Massachusetts. At first they worked on the widow's walk atop their house. Then her father built an observatory on the roof of the bank where he worked. Together they used a sextant to measure the angle between stars and the earth. At age twelve she recorded the seconds while her father observed a solar eclipse through a telescope.

When she grew up, Maria Mitchell worked as a librarian to support herself, but her heart was in astronomy. She continued watching the stars from the observatory atop the bank and in 1847 discovered the comet that made her famous. The next year she was elected to the American Academy of Arts and Sciences as its first woman member.

For someone so well-known, she was very humble. She said she had always liked mathematics, but she gave much of the credit for her success to her environment. In Nantucket knowledge of the stars was important for life at sea, so "people quite generally are in the habit of observing the heavens."

Maria Mitchell became a member of the first faculty at Vassar College, a new school for women, in 1865. She soon became one of the school's best loved and finest teachers. She displeased some people at the college when she refused to give grades. She felt strongly that "you cannot mark [grade] the human mind." She also started the American Association for the Advancement of Women as part of her long campaign to convince people that women scientists were as good as men.

Maria Mitchell and Professor Mary Whitney pose with their telescope in the Vassar observatory. (1877.)

Harriet Tubman

Born: about 1820, Dorchester County, MD   Died: 1913, Auburn, NY

Harriet Tubman, on the left, stands with a few of the people she led to freedom. After she escaped, she made many trips back to Maryland to guide others out. (About 1850s.)

Harriet Tubman was a legend in her own time. Born a slave, she escaped to the North when she was about thirty years old. She spent the rest of her life helping other African Americans.

For many years Harriet Tubman lived the harsh life of a slave. At six the Maryland plantation where she and her family lived hired her out to another farm. There she was beaten, starved, and made to sleep on the cold floor without a blanket. She barely survived.

At thirteen she blocked the doorway of a store so that another slave could escape. The man chasing the fleeing slave hit her in the head with a metal weight, cracking her skull. She suffered sudden and unexpected sleeping spells for the rest of her life. She occasionally fell asleep while leading others to freedom.

Twenty-eight slaves flee from the eastern shore of Maryland to freedom. Thousands of slaves risked their lives to escape. The Underground Railroad helped many along the way.

When Harriet Tubman's owner died in 1849, she heard that she would be sold to a chain gang bound for the deep South. She knew that life for slaves there was even worse than in Maryland, so she escaped to the North and freedom. Instead of staying safely there, she returned to Maryland at least eleven times during the next eight years and led others north. She helped so many slaves escape that she earned the name the "Moses of her people."

Even though slaveholders offered a $40,000 reward for her capture, she always escaped. She once disguised herself as an old woman selling chickens to avoid capture. Another time she confused slave hunters by boarding a train heading away from her destination.

Harriet Tubman's bravery continued during the Civil War. She served as a scout and a nurse. She also spied for the North by collecting information from African Americans living in Confederate territory. After the war she supported orphans and old people and worked to give African Americans the education she never had.

Slave-labor was more important than ever in the South when cotton became a major cash crop during the 1800s.

Harriet Beecher Stowe helped bring the evils of slavery to public attention in her book Uncle Tom's Cabin. *It was in many ways the most important book of the century. (1859.)*

Harriet Beecher Stowe

Born: 1811, Litchfield, CT   Died: 1896, Hartford, CT

"So you are the little woman who wrote the book that made this great war," President Abraham Lincoln said to Harriet Beecher Stowe when he met her in 1862. He meant that her novel, *Uncle Tom's Cabin*, was so powerful at showing the inhumanity of slavery that it helped start the Civil War.

Harriet Beecher was a small, dreamy child. Her father was a prominent Congregational minister. Her mother was model of Christian piety who died when Harriet was four. The family's life was full of reading and discussions about the

66

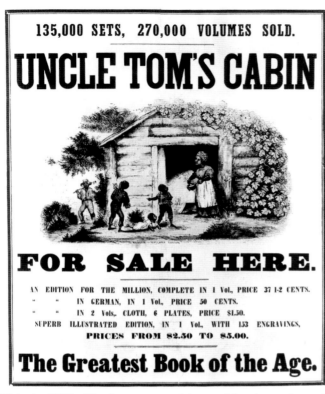

135,000 SETS, 270,000 VOLUMES SOLD.

UNCLE TOM'S CABIN

FOR SALE HERE.

AN EDITION FOR THE MILLION, COMPLETE IN 1 Vol., PRICE 37 1-2 CENTS.
"   "   IN GERMAN, IN 1 Vol., PRICE 50 CENTS.
"   "   IN 2 Vols., CLOTH, 6 PLATES, PRICE $1.50.
SUPERB ILLUSTRATED EDITION, IN 1 Vol., WITH 153 ENGRAVINGS,
PRICES FROM $2.50 TO $5.00.

The Greatest Book of the Age.

proper way to search for salvation. Her oldest sister, Catharine, took care of the children, started several schools, and later wrote books for women about running a household and raising children.

Uncle Tom's Cabin sold more than 300,000 copies in the United States during 1852 and just as many in other countries. It was the first wildly popular book in America.

Catharine and another sister, Mary, left home in 1823 to found the Hartford Female Seminary. Harriet began teaching there when she was sixteen. The family moved to Cincinnati, Ohio in 1832. Harriet wrote articles and books and taught in a school that Catharine founded there.

Four years later Harriet married and settled into family life. Although devoted to her children, she felt like a "domestic slave" and wrote and sold stories to magazines so that she could afford to hire household help. When Harriet was pregnant with her seventh child in 1850, the Stowes moved to Brunswick, Maine.

Chapters of *Uncle Tom's Cabin* began to appear in an anti-slavery newspaper in Washington, D.C. the next year. Harriet Beecher Stowe's hatred of slavery flowed from the pages. The three or four chapters she had planned grew into more than forty. When the series ended in 1852, *Uncle Tom's Cabin* was published as a book. Suddenly Harriet Beecher Stowe was famous.

Henry James, the great novelist, must not have realized that Harriet Beecher Stowe had been writing for almost twenty years when the novel was published. He wrote enviously: "At one step she has reached the top of the staircase up which the rest of us climb on our knees year after year." He might have added that through *Uncle Tom's Cabin*, Harriet Beecher Stowe brought the institution of slavery closer to its end.

An African-American slave is sold away from his wife and child. Family separation is a major theme of Uncle Tom's Cabin. *(1863.)*

THE PARTING "Buy us too."

Mary Ann Shadd Cary worked hard to end slavery.

Mary Ann Shadd Cary

Born: 1823, Wilmington, DE   Died: 1893, Washington, D.C.

Mary Ann Shadd Cary was the first African-American woman to edit a newspaper in North America and the first to win a law degree in the United States. She devoted her life to campaigning for African-American freedom and women's suffrage.

Born into a family of free blacks, Mary Ann Shadd Cary grew up in an atmosphere of action. Her father helped slaves escape to Canada along the Underground Railroad. At ten she began studying at a Quaker school in Pennsylvania. At sixteen she returned to Wilmington and started a private school for African Americans.

The Fugitive Slave Law of 1850 changed her life. The law stated that all escaped slaves living in free states could be returned to their owners. This drove many escapees to Canada where United States laws could not touch them. To collect rewards slave hunters sometimes captured free blacks and claimed that they were escaped slaves, so Mary Ann Shadd Cary and a brother joined the migration and settled across the border from Detroit in Windsor, Ontario.

Mary Ann Shadd Cary started writing soon after. Her pamphlet encouraging African Americans to move to Canada had such a zealous, effective style that she was asked to write newspaper articles. She was soon the editor of a newspaper designed to attract African Americans to Canada and help them find a place in Canadian society.

Mary Ann Shadd Cary traveled the United States in 1855-56 to deliver biting speeches against slavery. During the Civil War she worked to end slavery by recruiting African-American soldiers for the Union Army.

After the war she moved to Washington D.C. where she worked as a school principal for seventeen years. She studied law at Howard University Law School at the same time and was soon an outspoken lawyer. She spent the rest of her life campaigning for African-American equality and women's rights. She argued for her right to vote as an African-American resident of the District of Columbia before the Judiciary Committee of the House of Representatives. She won her case and became one of a handful of American women to vote in the United States.

An African-American teacher instructs a class. Mary Ann Shadd Cary and other African Americans knew that education was key to gaining influence in America. (1870.)

Women of the Civil War

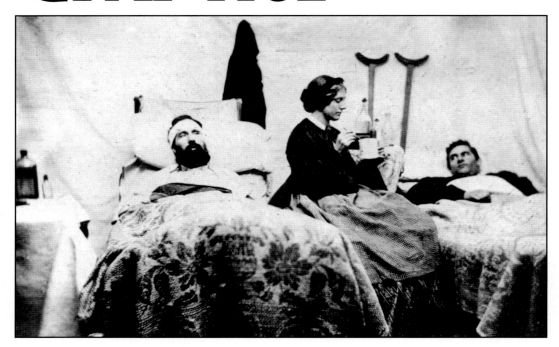

A woman nurse tends a patient at a Union hospital in Tennessee during the Civil War. Nurses saved thousands whom infection would have killed.

Everywhere the grass had been moistened with blood . . . everywhere wounded men were lying in the streets on heaps of blood-stained straw. . . . They lay like trees uprooted by a tornado . . . sick with the pains of wounds, grim with the dust of long marches and the smoke and powder of battle, looking up with wild haggard faces.

Sophronia Bucklin wrote these lines after the battle at Gettysburg, where more than 50,000 men were killed or wounded. Stirred by the war "to do and dare," she left her job as a seamstress in Auburn, New York to become an army nurse.

When the war began, few people thought women would or should be directly involved. War was considered "no place for a woman" and nursing no job for a woman. Women were expected to stay home, tend family, farms, and businesses, work in factories or shops, and roll bandages. Even so, a sense of duty motivated hundreds of women to follow the army and serve as cooks, laundresses, seamstresses, and nurses. Betsy Sullivan, called "Mother Sullivan" by the First Tennessee Infantry Regiment, traveled with her husband. She stepped into battles to wrap wounds and distribute water. She even went to prison with her husband when he was wounded and captured. Another woman, Catherine Oliphant, received a tribute from the Third Maryland Cavalry: "While she enrolled as a laundress, she served, in fact, as an army nurse."

As deaths and losses mounted, accepting women as nurses seemed the only way to care for wounded and ill soldiers. Thousands of women answered the call. Dorothea Dix organized the Army Nursing Corps for the Union. It was the first professional nursing service in the United States. Dix's nurses earned $12 a month. Doctors earned between $100 and $169 a month. Many nurses lived rugged lives, sleeping in hallways and tents, eating when and what they could. Sophronia Bucklin wrote:

> We endured the cold without sufficient bedding for our hard beds. . . . On bitter mornings we rose shivering, broke the ice in our pails, and washed our numb hands and faces, then went out into the raw air, up to our mess room, also without fire, thence to the wards.

Frances L. Clalin poses in a Union cavalry uniform.

What did men think of women in medicine? Some military men sent all women nurses away and said that there was no work for them. Others accepted women as long as they were "feminine" and did not interfere with the physicians' authority. Few men consented to work with one of the war's few woman physicians, Dr. Mary Walker, who always wore trousers. Assigned to a regiment in Tennessee, Dr. Walker acted as both physician and spy, gathering information for the Union while tending sick civilians in the area. She was arrested, imprisoned, and eventually freed in exchange for a Confederate officer.

Women also fought. More than four hundred women disguised themselves as men and became soldiers. "Frank Martin" was wounded at Murfreesboro, discovered to be a woman, and discharged. When she recovered, she enlisted in another regiment where she was also found out. Jennie Hodgers served three years with the Ninety-fifth Illinois Infantry Regiment as Albert Cashier and lived the next fifty years disguised as a man. Some women became smugglers. Alicia Buckner was nicknamed the "Fair Apothecary" for trying to cross from the North to the South with nine pounds of medicine hidden under her skirts. Another woman attempted to smuggle twelve pairs of boots crammed with medicine and whiskey into the South.

When the war ended, many women who had worked for the war effort returned to their old lives. Others continued with careers they had started during the war. Women had again proved themselves in the world outside the home. They had also succeeded in creating a new profession, nursing, which women still dominate.

Women on the Home Front

A girl reads in front of a cabin in Aiken, South Carolina. Before the Civil War teaching slaves to read had been against the law because reading spread ideas and helped slaves escape. After the war many African Americans still lived in poverty, but they were finally free and could legally learn to read. (Photo by J.A. Palmer, 1876.)

Most women stayed at home during the war. They added the work of the men away at war to their own, just as women had during the American Revolution. Women in both the North and the South also set up and ran more than 20,000 Soldiers' Aid Societies. These organizations collected medical supplies, knitted, and sent food packages to soldiers. Many societies also raised money for the war effort. One in New York City collected more than a million dollars at one event.

Some northern women who stayed home worked in factories making cartridges, shoes, and textiles. Many southern women had a hard time finding jobs. Some worked in the Confederate Clothing Bureau in Richmond, Virginia and earned thirty cents for each shirt they made. A few lucky ones landed jobs with the Confederate Treasury Department and earned six times the wage of an army private.

Women in the South felt the war more than those in the North. Many of them wore shoes with wooden soles and wrote letters on wall paper. Some did not have enough money to feed and clothe their families. Sometimes southern women were so desperate that they broke the law. One group stole twenty barrels of flour during a Richmond food riot in 1863. Another looted food warehouses in Salisbury, North Carolina. Nearly 300,000 Southerners fled their homes as Union armies invaded the South during the last years of the war. Sometimes the advancing soldiers took everything, and families starved to death.

African-American women of the South suffered most of all. Thousands tried to escape, and many succeeded. One seventy-

two-year-old slave from Georgia led her clan of twenty-two children and grandchildren down the Savannah River by barge to freedom. Some waited for the Union Army to free them. Lydie Penney left the countryside for Memphis and stayed there until the army entered the city. Then she worked as nurse for the troops. Amy Spain was not so lucky. She was hung by slave owners in South Carolina for yelling, "Bless the Lord, the Yankees have come."

The Soldiers' Aid Society of Springfield, Illinois displays some of the food and clothing it is preparing to send to Union troops. (About 1863.)

Southern women had encouraged their husbands, fathers, and brothers to fight when the war broke out. After four years of war, they wrote letters filled with hardship. Twenty percent of the South's army deserted and headed home to help provide for their desperate families. Almost a million southern soldiers were dead by the last year of the war. Eighty thousand women were widows in Alabama alone.

After the war the South lay in ruin and poverty while the North experienced economic growth and prosperity. Most southern white women longed for the stability and prosperity of the past. Only a few of them pressed for the vote or better jobs. African Americans were free, but good jobs and quality education lay far in the future for them. They spent years struggling to end the legacies left by two centuries of slavery.

Before the war many northern women had campaigned to abolish slavery and win the vote for themselves. After the Civil War they thought that they should be rewarded for their help by gaining the right to vote. Northern men were willing to grant African-American men the vote, but most of them were against women's suffrage. The Fourteenth and Fifteenth Amendments to the Constitution granted non-white men the right to vote, but it said nothing about women. Many women were disappointed, just as their great-great-grandmothers had been after the American Revolution. They did not go home and wait quietly, though. Instead they took up new kinds of jobs and pressed harder than ever for the right to vote.

Elizabeth Blackwell

Born: 1821, England   Died: 1910, England

For centuries women in America had practiced medicine as midwives, herbalists, and shamans. Over time, however, colleges and medical schools gained more and more control over the medical profession, and women were shut out. Elizabeth Blackwell began the march of women back into professional medicine by becoming the first woman in the United States trained in a medical school.

Born in England of parents who believed in women's rights, Elizabeth Blackwell and her sisters and brothers were educated at home by tutors. The family moved to the United States in 1832. Six years later Mr. Blackwell died. Elizabeth, her mother, and two older sisters started a school to support the family. Disappointed that "ennobling companionship" was missing from her relationships with men, she resolved not to marry. She instead followed a friend's advice and decide to become a doctor.

Elizabeth Blackwell's ground-breaking work brought women back into medicine, a field they had once dominated as midwives and herbalists. (1840s.)

Even though Elizabeth Blackwell was well-educated and intelligent, she had a hard time finding a medical school that would accept her. Medical students usually came from colleges that excluded women, so medical colleges could always say that women were unqualified.

Elizabeth Blackwell had a strange piece of luck. She applied to Geneva Medical College in New York state, and the all male class was allowed to decide her fate. Because they thought her application was a hoax by a rival school, the students voted to accept her. Much to their surprise and dismay a woman arrived to join their class.

At first they treated her rudely and did not allow her into the classroom, but gradually some of the students and faculty came to admire her intelligence and dedication. She graduated in 1849, first in her class. Afterward, a Philadelphia hospital allowed her to continue her training on its wards, even though many of the other physicians did not want her there.

Against tremendous odds Elizabeth Blackwell had turned a class joke into a great achievement and become the first woman in the United States to earn a degree as a physician. Despite her excellence, Geneva Medical College was not inspired to train other women. The year she finished, the college ruled not to accept applications from women.

Elizabeth Blackwell dedicated the rest of her life to women's health and to helping women advance in medicine. After going to Europe for further training, Dr. Blackwell settled in New York. During the next two decades, she set up a clinic for poor women, a hospital, and a medical school for women. She was soon joined in her work by her younger sister, Dr. Emily Blackwell, who had trained at the medical college of Western Reserve University in Cleveland and was a skilled doctor and administrator.

Dr. Elizabeth Blackwell moved back to England in 1869 and soon had a thriving practice. She lectured widely on hygiene and morality and became an internationally recognized physician. She was named Chair of Gynecology at the New Hospital and London School of Medicine for Women in 1875. Her courage and determination re-opened the professional practice of medicine to women.

The anatomical lecture room at the Medical College for Women in New York. Dr. Blackwell started the school in 1868 because most medical colleges that trained men refused to admit women and the two medical schools already established for women did not meet her high standards. (1870.)

Susan B. Anthony & Elizabeth Cady Stanton

Anthony—
Born: 1820, Adams, MA
Died: 1906, Rochester, NY
Stanton—
Born: 1815, Johnstown, NY
Died: 1902, New York, NY

Susan B. Anthony and Elizabeth Cady Stanton stood at the center of the nineteenth century movement for women's suffrage. Susan B. Anthony was raised in a Quaker home where women and men were regarded as equal before God. She came to believe that women should also have equality in the political world.

Anthony taught for several years in Quaker schools. When she returned home to manage the family farm, she became politically active. She joined abolitionist and temperance movements that worked to end slavery and ban alcoholic beverages. When she was denied the right to speak at a temperance rally because she was a woman, women's rights and suffrage became her main focus.

Susan B. Anthony's path was often difficult. Some opponents made fun of the way she looked. One newspaperman wrote that she was "personally repulsive." Another called her "lean, cadaverous, and intellectual." Her enthusiasm and ability never wavered. They became even stronger after she met Elizabeth Cady Stanton.

When Elizabeth Cady Stanton was a child, her only brother died. "Oh, my daughter, I wish you were a boy," her father told her. Then and there she resolved to prove that girls were as capable and important as boys. She studied Greek,

Elizabeth Cady Stanton, on the left, and Susan B. Anthony spearheaded the nineteenth century campaign to win the vote for women.

Latin, and mathematics, subjects usually restricted to college-bound boys. Then she attended Emma Willard's Troy Female Seminary to learn even more.

She married in 1840, and the newlyweds took a honeymoon trip to England because her husband was a delegate to the world's anti-slavery convention in London. Lucretia Mott, a woman delegate from the United States, and women delegates from other countries were forbidden to speak before the gathering. They were even denied the right to set foot on the convention floor. To hear the debate Elizabeth Cady Stanton and the other women had to sit behind a screen so that no one could see them.

This strengthened Elizabeth Cady Stanton's resolve to work for women's equality. She, Lucretia Mott, and several other women organized the first women's rights convention. It was held in 1848 at Seneca Falls, New York. The conference passed Stanton's Declaration of Sentiments, which demanded that women be allowed to vote.

Elizabeth Cady Stanton and Susan B. Anthony met in 1850 and became immediate friends and allies in the crusade for women's rights. Stanton eventually bore seven children, but she continued to write articles, travel, and lecture. Anthony kept working, too. She traveled continually, often slogging through mud and snow to give speeches. Sometimes Anthony even went from house to house to win supporters.

Often Stanton and Anthony traveled and campaigned together. In 1869 they established the National Woman Suffrage Association, an organization committed to winning the vote for women. Stanton was president of the organization for twenty-three years. Anthony was president for eighteen years after Stanton stepped down.

Women suffragists flood the Capitol in 1916. They are determined to convince Congress to pass a constitutional amendment giving women the vote. Anthony and Stanton helped start the march toward the Nineteenth Amendment, which was finally passed almost seventy years after the two met. (1916.)

"Failure is impossible," Anthony reminded suffragists. She was right. Although neither Anthony nor Stanton lived to see the victory, their efforts led to the Nineteenth Amendment to the United States Constitution. Ratified in 1920, it gave women the right to vote in all elections.

Belva Lockwood ran for president of the United States in 1884 and 1888 as the National Equal Rights Party candidate.

Belva Lockwood

Born: 1830, Royalton, NY   Died: 1917, Washington D.C.

Belva Lockwood overcame many barriers to become the first woman to practice law before the United States Supreme Court.

Born and raised on a farm, she quit school at fifteen to teach. She married four years later and had to give up her job. Her husband soon died, and she began teaching again to support herself and her young daughter. She had always wanted a better education, so she went to college at the same time and graduated with honors. In 1866 she moved to Washington D.C. where she opened one of that city's first private school for both girls and boys.

When she was almost forty years old, Belva Lockwood decided to change careers. She had been reading law on her own for some time. Now she decided to become a practicing lawyer. She applied to three law schools in Washington, D.C., but they all rejected her because she was a woman. One even said that the male students wouldn't be able to concentrate with a woman around.

Finally the new National University Law School agreed to accept her, but when she finished in 1873, the school would not give her a diploma. She wrote to Ulysses S. Grant, the president of the United States, who was also the unofficial president of the school, and demanded her diploma. She received it and began practicing law, but more obstacles lay ahead. She was preparing to argue a case

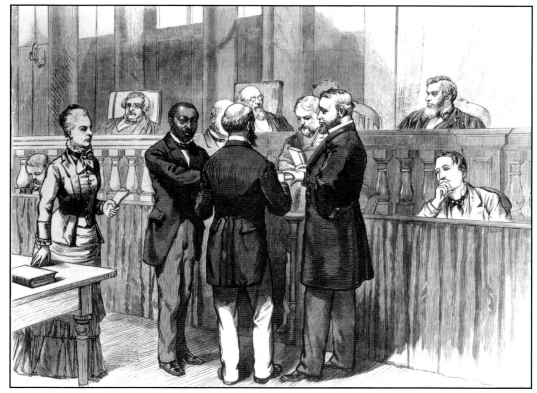

Belva Lockwood was serious about equal rights. Only a year after she received the right to practice law before the Supreme Court, she sponsored Samuel Lowery, an African-American lawyer, for admission to the Court. (1880.)

before the United States Court of Claims when the court told her that she could not because she was a woman. A request to plead before the United States Supreme Count was also denied.

Belva Lockwood took action. She wrote a law allowing women to practice law before the Supreme Court. Then she convinced a few powerful United States Senators to support it. When the law was passed in 1879, the Court of Claims had no choice but to change its policy, too. She had won two major battles and opened the way for women to practice before both courts.

During her long career as a lawyer, she also was involved in other important cases. In one of them, she won a five million dollar suit against the United States government for the Eastern Cherokee people.

The obstacles Belva Lockwood faced made her a strong advocate for human rights. She campaigned widely for women's suffrage, equal rights, and equal pay. She even ran for president. She was still campaigning and lecturing when she died at age eighty-seven.

BELVA A. LOCKWOOD

PLATFORM
OF THE
NATIONAL EQUAL RIGHTS PARTY.

1. We pledge ourselves, if elected to power, so far as in us lies, to do equal and exact justice to every class of our citizens, without distinction of color, sex, or nationality.

Belva Lockwood also wrote the platform for the National Equal Rights Party. "We pledge ourselves . . . to do equal and exact justice to every class of our citizens, without distinction of color, sex, or nationality."

Sarah Winnemucca

Born: 1844, Humboldt Sink, NV   Died: 1891, Monida, MT

Sarah Winnemucca was photographed in the finery she wore when she toured the country to talk about the plight of Native Americans.

When whites massacred Native Americans and pushed them onto reservations after the Civil War, Sarah Winnemucca, the daughter and granddaughter of Paiute chiefs, began a struggle for Indian rights. This earned her the name "Mother" from the Paiute people.

Hatred for Native Americans was not new to Sarah Winnemucca. As a child she went with her grandfather to California to work on a ranch and quickly learned English and Spanish. Before her grandfather died, he made the family promise to send his bright granddaughter to school at Saint Mary's Convent in San Jose, California. His wishes were obeyed, but Sarah Winnemucca was dismissed after only three weeks. The parents of white students did not want their children going to school with an Indian.

When Sarah Winnemucca was a young woman, the United States Army and white settlers who came into Nevada forced the Paiutes onto a reservation. Then the Paiute people were driven into poverty and famine by dishonest government agents. Angry and starving Paiute warriors stole some cattle from the settlers. In retaliation soldiers slaughtered Paiute women, children, and old people while the warriors of the tribe were away hunting. One of Sarah Winnemucca's brothers was killed.

After a year of famine and death, many Paiutes went to an army post for food. Since Sarah Winnemucca knew Spanish, English, and three Native American languages, she acted as an interpreter for her people. Because she was so skillful,

Paiute Indians in Nevada. (Photo by Timothy H. O'Sullivan, 1871.)

the government soon hired her as an interpreter and guide. In 1878, during the Bannock Wars between the army and the Bannock Indians, Sarah Winnemucca traveled alone through a hundred miles of rough terrain to rescue her father and some of his band.

After the wars the Paiutes were as desperate and poor as before. Sarah Winnemucca gave speeches about their plight and mistreatment. She and other Native Americans went to Washington to meet with President Rutherford B. Hayes and the United States Secretary of the Interior. The Indians were promised more land. When the land was not handed over, Sarah Winnemucca set out on a speaking tour to tell people about the hardships faced by Native Americans. She sold the book she had written about her life to pay expenses. Because of her long hair and Paiute dress, white audiences called her "The Princess." Progress was slow, but Sarah Winnemucca kept working for her people her whole life.

Southern Paiute women carry water.
(Photo by John K. Hillers, 1872.)

Matilda Coxe Stevenson stands third from the right with her back to the camera at a Zuni Pueblo. She and other anthropologists wanted to study Native American customs before white settlement changed them. (Photo by Ben Wittick, 1896.)

Matilda Coxe Stevenson

Born: 1849, San Augustine, TX   Died: 1915, Oxon Hill, MD

As the century progressed, more and more women worked at jobs traditionally open only to men. Matilda Coxe Stevenson was one of them. She was the first woman anthropologist in the United States, and she looked at Native American cultures in a new way.

Matilda moved to Washington D.C. when she was an infant and went to school in Philadelphia. Soon after her marriage in 1872, she traveled to a Zuni pueblo in New Mexico with her geologist husband and two anthropologists. What she saw gave her life a new focus.

Matilda Coxe Stevenson helped her husband with his work in New Mexico. Although she did not receive credit for her assistance, she used the opportunity to learn the best ways to study native cultures. Soon she struck out on her own, observing and writing about Zuni women, children, and religion. She was the first

Matilda Coxe Stevenson, on the right, with her husband and two other men rest at their camp in Canyon de Chelly, Arizona. They recorded Native American customs and collected artifacts for the Smithsonian Institution in Washington, D.C. (Photo by Ben Wittick, 1882.)

anthropologist in the United States to realize that the way children are raised has a profound impact on a society. Her work also brought her face to face with adventure. Once she was held captive in a kiva or underground chamber by Hopi Indians when she watched a secret ceremony.

Because she was a woman and because most anthropologists did not understand how important women and children were to cultures, her work was ignored. When a famous anthropologist praised her contributions, she and her work were suddenly appreciated and respected.

She established the Women's Anthropological Society of America in 1885. Five years later she felt that she could dissolve the society, because women were among the first members of the new American Anthropological Association. She published her most important work in 1904. It was a six hundred page study of Zuni religion

and ceremony. During her later years she lived among the Tewa at San Ildefonso pueblo in New Mexico, where the young Maria Martinez (see 1900s) knew her.

Matilda Coxe Stevenson was a remarkable woman in a man's field. She introduced a new area of study in American anthropology and blazed the way for other women to enter a profession closed to them in the past.

Matilda Coxe Stevenson took this photo of two sisters who were the best pottery artists at the Zia pueblo in New Mexico. She and the other anthropologists in her group were among the first people to record Native American culture with cameras. (About 1888.)

1900 The United States population tops 76 million. More than 9 million immigrants enter the country during the next ten years.

1908 The first Model T cars are made. They sell for $850. By 1926 the cost is down to $350.

1916 Jeanette Rankin of Montana becomes the first woman elected to the United States Congress.

1917-1918 The United States fights in World War I, which began in Europe in 1914.

1920 The Nineteenth Amendment to the Constitution is passed. It gives women the right to vote in all elections.

1929-1939 The Great Depression. By 1932, 12 million people are out of work in the country.

1941-1945 The United States fights in World War II, which began in Europe in 1939.

1900   **1925**

1900s

More women than ever before were graduating from college by the end of the twentieth century. About eighteen percent of America's women had attended college for four or more years by 1999, compared with about six percent in 1960. (Wellesley College Graduation, 1997.)

1961 The birth control pill, nicknamed "the pill," comes into wide use.

1958 Passenger jet service begins, and the first United States satellite goes into orbit.

1961-1973 The war with Vietnam sparks discontent at home.

1968 Shirley Chisholm of New York becomes the first African-American women elected to Congress.

1969 The United States lands the first man on the moon.

1975 The first personal computer is developed.

1980s The AIDS epidemic hits the US.

1990 The nation's population reaches 272 million.

1950

1975

2000

Young workers stand outside a factory in this 1910 photo by Lewis Hine. His photographs of working children during the early 1900s shocked the country.

Women's Work

Business and industry continued to boom during the early 1900s. Almost half the people in the United States lived in cities, and twenty percent of the paid workers were women. They earned money at home sewing shirts and making paper flowers. They earned money in factories sorting rags, canning food, sewing, and wiring appliances. They worked as nurses, teachers, typists, domestics, and sales clerks.

Women with jobs worked hard. One factory owner said he hired women immigrants when he could, because "they keep at it like horses." Sales clerks spent most of their sixty to eighty hour workweek on their feet and earned between six and seven dollars. Women and children who made paper flowers in crowded apartments received ten cents for every 144 flowers.

Wages for working women averaged $5.25 a week in 1905, less than half the amount for men. Higher paying jobs were usually closed to women. When a woman was lucky enough to land one, she was paid from one-third to one-half as much as the men who did the same work. A few women were wildly successful. One was Madame C. J. Walker, an African American. She started a hair care and cosmetics company with $1.50 in 1905 and became the first American woman to earn a million dollars.

Working conditions and wages were often so miserable that women formed unions. The International Ladies' Garment Workers' Union, led more than 20,000 shirtwaist workers out on strike in 1909. Women with more money tried to help, too. Guided by Jane Addams of Chicago, they opened settlement houses to feed poor native-born and immigrant families. They wrote about the wretched conditions of working families and campaigned for laws to improve factories and housing. Well-to-do Bessie Van Vorst took a job in a Pittsburgh canning factory to see what it was like. She found the work exhausting and the pay low.

I have stood ten hours; I have fitted 1,300 corks; I have hauled and loaded 4,000 jars of pickles. My pay is seventy cents.

Women who looked for jobs early in the second half of the century found that their pay still averaged less than half the amount that men earned. They lobbied to correct the unfairness. New laws were passed in the mid-1960s saying that women and men must be paid the same amount for the same work and that women and minorities must have a chance at all jobs. The new laws helped close the gap, but problems remained.

Margie Cunha lived in poverty until she landed a traditional "man's job." She pestered a coal company for work just when the United States government was pressuring the company to obey the new laws and hire women miners. After a demanding physical test, she became a coal miner and began working 810 feet underground. The high wages she earned turned her life around.

By the century's end women had made outstanding gains. Almost half the wage earners in the country were women, and more women than ever were entering the business world. Estee Lauder started a cosmetics business in her kitchen during the 1940s. Fifty years later it was among the 400 richest companies in the country. When Carleton "Carly" Fiorina was named chief executive officer of Hewlett-Packard in 1999, she became the first woman to head a major American computer company.

Even so, as the century ended far fewer women than men were bosses. Only three women headed Fortune 500 companies, America's largest businesses. Working women also earned only $77 for every $100 earned by working men. A woman who graduated from college could expect to make $2000 a year less than a man who had finished high school.

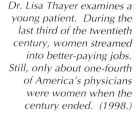

Dr. Lisa Thayer examines a young patient. During the last third of the twentieth century, women streamed into better-paying jobs. Still, only about one-fourth of America's physicians were women when the century ended. (1998.)

An African American serves dinner to a white family in Kansas during the early part of the century. African Americans and immigrants often worked as domestic servants and laundresses, because few other jobs were open to them. Domestics earned room, board, and $2-5 per week for 12-14 hour workdays. Laundresses made about 50 cents a day, roughly half the amount earned by women working in other fields. (About 1907.)

Women's Place

During the twentieth century American women marched toward equality. When the century began, thousands of women were busy following the lead of nineteenth century activists who had pushed for women's suffrage. Many worked through the National American Woman Suffrage Association (NAWSA). They paraded in the streets, gave speeches, wrote articles, and hounded Congress.

In 1919 Congress finally proposed an amendment to the Constitution that would allow women to vote. By the next summer only one more state needed to approve the amendment for it to become law. Carrie Chapman Catt, president of the NAWSA, spent two months in Tennessee trying to convince the all-male legislature to pass the amendment. Her effort paid off. On August 18, 1920, Tennessee voted in favor of suffrage for women by one vote. The Nineteenth Amendment to the Constitution became law eight days later, and women could finally vote in all elections.

Women post a sign high enough for everyone to see. They are advertising a speech in New Jersey by Dr. Anna Howard Shaw, the president of the National American Woman Suffrage Association from 1904 to 1915.

During the 1960s women became politically active again. It was an explosive time in America. African Americans marched for civil rights. Many people were angry about the Vietnam War, because men who were too young to vote were dying for a cause they did not understand. Many women supported civil rights for African Americans and campaigned to end the Vietnam War, but they also demanded equality for their gender. More women than ever were part of the paid labor force. They worked hard and were well trained and educated. They wanted the freedom to compete for any job. They wanted a voice in their country's government. They wanted lives outside the home.

People called them women's "libbers," since their slogan was "Women's Liberation." They marched in the streets and wrote articles and books. They ran for Congress and burned their bras to symbolize the restrictions that held them back.

Some women thought that the only way to win equality was through an Equal Rights Amendment to the United States Constitution that said women and men were equal under the law. Some people were afraid that the Equal Rights Amendment would take away hard-won improvements in working conditions, force women to fight in wars, and end alimony payments for divorced women. The amendment did not pass.

Even so, women made huge strides during the second half of the century. New laws gave women the legal right to compete for any job, and the chance to go to better colleges, take out loans to start businesses, buy homes, and have medical leave from their jobs during childbirth.

Birth control made it possible for many women to take advantage of the new gains. Margaret Sanger, the pioneer for birth control in America, thought her mother had died at forty-nine because she was exhausted from bearing and caring for eleven children. She began telling women about birth control in 1912. Since birth control was against the law, she was sent to jail many times. She kept talking anyway.

A mother and daughter mix batter in 1955. After the Second World War many women left work and went back to caring for their families full time. But by 1997 sixty percent of America's women worked outside the home, compared with thirty-four percent in 1950.

Katherine Dexter McCormick followed in Margaret Sanger's footsteps forty years later. She believed that women could only be independent if they had children when they wanted them. She helped finance the research and development of the birth control pill, the most reliable method of birth control for women yet. Suddenly many women were free from unplanned pregnancies and could have lives beyond the home.

Today's women are more active in American life than ever before. They design buildings, manage offices, pave streets, sit in Congress, and conduct scientific research. More American women can make decisions about their lives than that at any time in history.

Women again march for equality in Washington, D.C., this time in 1970, fifty years after winning the vote.

Even in the twentieth century, working in the house, garden, and field was backbreaking for farm women. (1904.)

Mary Hamilton

Born: 1866, Randolph County, Illinois   Died: date and place unknown

Like half of America's women in the early twentieth century, Mary Hamilton lived on the land. Her life was spent moving from place to place, and she had to work as hard as most colonial women just to survive.

When Mary Hamilton was seventeen, her family moved from Missouri to Arkansas. Her father died of pneumonia a week after they arrived. Mary, her mother, and four other children started a boarding house to support themselves. Young Mary was the head cook. Pneumonia claimed Mary's mother and a brother a few months later. As the two lay near death, Mary promised them that she would marry an Englishman with a mysterious past who had vowed to take care of the younger children. Not long after her eighteenth birthday, she did.

Hard work and perseverance defined Mary Hamilton's life. After she married she again cooked in a boarding house, this time from four in the morning until nine at night. Every day she baked 115 loaves of bread, at least thirty pies, and countless biscuits and flapjacks to feed loggers who worked nearby. When her first

Mary Jane Clough and her daughter cook in Mrs. Clough's kitchen in Prescott, Arizona. Mary Hamilton cooked huge meals for loggers in kitchens much like this one. (About 1900.)

child was born, she turned him over to a nurse because she needed to keep cooking. He grew sick and died within a few months. Her second child was born a month early and died within hours. Her third died when a doctor accidentally gave it poison instead of medicine. Her fourth died, too, but her last four children lived and took care of their mother when she was old.

For most of her adult life, Mary Hamilton and her husband moved among the logging camps and farms of Mississippi and Arkansas, working and searching for a better life. She cooked for crews and also sewed. She sometimes earned a dollar a day by making a dress a day for women who lived nearby. When the family farmed, she added work in the fields to her regular household tasks. She went from cooking and washing to plowing and weeding without a pause.

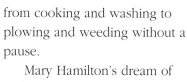

Mary Hamilton's dream of settling down permanently on a place of her own did not come true, and she was never famous. Even so, she found joy and pride in her family, her work, and the beauty of the countryside. Her gallant life was typical of women's lives during the first half of the century.

Some of the people who worked in lumber camps lived in small shacks like these. Others lived in tents. (1935.)

Rose Schneiderman

Born: 1882, Saven, Poland   Died: 1972, New York, NY

Even though Rose Schneiderman was only four feet, six inches tall, she was a dynamic speaker and effective union organizer.

Born into a poor tailor's family in Russian-occupied Poland, Rose Schneiderman became a crusader in the struggle to improve working conditions for wage-earning women in the United States.

When she was eight, Rose Schneiderman's family immigrated to New York City and lived in an apartment with one windowless bedroom. A sink in the hallway served all the apartments on the floor. Her father died less than two years later, and she was sent to an orphanage where the staff was cruel. Girls who disobeyed the rules were beaten or locked in a closet. Her mother found a job in a clothing factory the next year, and Rose Schneiderman came home. When Rose was thirteen, Mrs. Schneiderman lost her job, and the girl reluctantly quit school to become the wage-earner of the family. Bright and eager to learn, she had finished nine grades in four years of school.

At first Rose Schneiderman worked in a department store, earning $2.16 for a workweek of sixty-four hours. Three years later she was earning only sixty cents more, so she looked for a job that paid more.

Even though her mother considered factory work degrading and wanted something better for her daughter, Rose Schneiderman started sewing linings for men's caps in a factory. She had to supply her own sewing machine and thread, and once she and the other seamstresses lost their machines in a fire. Although the factory was insured, the sewing machines were not, so she and the other young women had to buy new ones. She stayed because the first week her pay envelope held six dollars, more than twice the amount she had earned before.

Still, a dollar a day was not much to live on, and a visit with a family in Montreal convinced her that belonging to a union was the only way to improve wages and working conditions. She and two other young women started a union at their factory in 1903. Managers had sped up the work, but cut the pay.

> We girls needed an organization [union]. The men had organized already and had gained some advantages, but the bosses lost nothing, as they took it out on us.

Two years later the young women won a thirteen-week strike. Rose Schneiderman spent the rest of her life working in the women's labor movement.

She soon joined the Women's Trade Union League. It was an organization with members from both the working class and upper class that struggled to improve the lives of working women. She became a union vice president the next year. While she worked for the WTUL, she traveled widely to win members for the International Ladies' Garment Worker's Union. It eventually became one of the strongest unions in the country. When fire broke out in 1911 at the Triangle Shirtwaist Factory, 146 women and girls died because they were locked inside. Rose Schneiderman's words about their deaths stirred the crowd.

> This is not the first time girls have been burned alive in the city. . . . Every year thousands of us are maimed. The life of men and women is so cheap and property is so sacred. There are so many of us for one job it matters little.

Rose Schneiderman was president of the New York Women's Trade Union League for thirty years. She was also president of the National Women's Trade Union League for twenty-five of those years. In spite of her success, she continued to live simply, dedicating all her energy to helping the working class and the poor.

Rose Schneiderman sews cap linings in this posed picture. She was a leader in the "Uprising of the 20,000," when workers from more than five hundred shirtwaist factories walked away from their jobs. One of their banners read: "WE ARE STARVING WHILE WE WORK, WE MIGHT AS WELL STARVE WHILE WE STRIKE." (1908.)

This dim, crowded mailbag repair shop in Washington, D.C. was typical of sewing sweatshops. They were usually unhealthy and often dangerous. (1907.)

Maria Martinez, at San Ildefonso in about 1941, builds pottery from coils made of red clay and very fine blue sand.

Maria Martinez

Born: about 1887, San Ildefonso, NM   Died: 1980, San Ildefonso, NM

When Maria Martinez's aunt lifted the girl's first piece of pottery from the fire, she predicted that her niece would always have good luck with her pottery. Her prediction came true. Maria Martinez became a potter of international fame. From all over the world people visited the dry New Mexico countryside to watch her make pottery and to buy her creations.

Maria Martinez grew up much like other girls at San Ildefonso in New Mexico. She traded the cheese her mother made to other women in the village. She participated in Pueblo ceremonies and dances. She learned to care for the household and went to school. More than anything else, she and one of her sisters liked to play in the miniature adobe houses they built beside the irrigation ditch next to their home. When the girls began eating lunch in the playhouses, young Maria decided that they should make dishes from the clay found in the ditch. The dishes always broke as they dried, so the sisters asked an aunt to teach them to make pottery, the same way that dozens of Pueblo women would one day ask Maria Martinez.

Even though Maria Martinez tried to live a typical life, she became different. An archaeologist asked her to make a pot like one dug up in an ancient Indian village. She made several pots, and her husband, Julian Martinez, painted designs on them. The archaeologist bought some for the Indian Museum in Santa Fe, and a merchant sold others in his shop. The pots were very popular. People wanted to buy more. Maria Martinez made other pots and other kinds of pottery, too. Most of the pottery was colored cream, red, and black.

Maria and Julian Martinez developed a new style of pottery in about 1920. It had a shiny black background with designs in matte or unshiny black. The style made Maria famous. People wanted to buy it faster than she could craft it.

Maria Martinez was always humble about her talents. She said her pottery was no better than that of her neighbors. To Maria Martinez being a part of the Pueblo was more important than being an internationally known potter.

Maria Martinez uses a scraper to smooth the coils of a pot in 1950. The thin, hard walls made her pottery special.

She always fired her pottery outside. Building the fire so that the pieces baked correctly was part of the art. (About 1950.)

A crowd welcomes Amelia Earhart to Ireland on May 21, 1932 after her 2,000 mile flight across the Atlantic Ocean. The United States Congress awarded her the Distinguished Flying Cross for the feat.

Amelia Earhart

Born: 1897, Atchison, KS   Disappeared: 1937, Pacific Ocean

Amelia Earhart won instant fame in 1928 when she became the first woman to cross the Atlantic Ocean in an airplane. Even though she kept the logbook instead of flying the plane, people considered her a hero. Four years later she was a hero again when she became the first woman to fly across the Atlantic Ocean alone.

Amelia Earhart always had a head for adventure. She embraced life and tackled everything she could. She jumped fences on her way home from school, to the dismay of her grandmother who considered it unladylike. Earhart and her sister once built a wooden roller coaster. Their mother made them take it down after Earhart crashed eight feet to the ground in the wooden box the girls used as their car. When she grew up, Amelia Earhart said, "I think it is just about the most important thing a girl can do—try herself out, do something."

When the United States entered World War I in 1917, Amelia Earhart went to work as a nurse. The stories that injured pilots told about flying made her want to be a pilot, too. When the war ended she found "a top-notch flier" who was a woman to teach her. She flew solo for the first time in 1921.

Amelia Earhart used her fame to speak out about women and society. "Wages should be based on work, not sex nor any other consideration," she said. She married in 1931, but she did not accept the widespread view of marriage. "I believe that both men and women should be in the home some of the time, and out some of the time. Fifty-fifty."

Amelia Earhart never stopped flying. She was the first person to fly alone from Hawaii to the mainland United States. She and a navigator set out on a flight around the world in 1937. Near the end of the trip, they vanished over the Pacific Ocean. The public was shocked and sad. People have searched for the plane's wreckage ever since.

Amelia Earhart set many records for speed and distance during her brief career. She was also a founder and the first president of the Ninety-Nines, an organization of licensed women pilots that still exists.

Amelia Earhart in 1921, the year of her first solo flight.

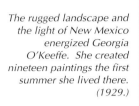
The rugged landscape and the light of New Mexico energized Georgia O'Keeffe. She created nineteen paintings the first summer she lived there. (1929.)

Georgia O'Keeffe

Born: 1887, Sun Prairie, WI   Died: 1986, Sante Fe, NM

Georgia O'Keeffe became one of the most famous American artists in history. Raised in Wisconsin and Virginia, she decided at age twelve that she wanted to become a painter. At eighteen she began studying at the Art Institute of Chicago. When she visited her family in Virginia that summer, she became ill with typhoid fever. After she recovered she studied at New York's Art Students League, then taught art in schools in several states while she continued to study and paint.

A personal artistic breakthrough changed her work and made her famous. In 1915 Georgia O'Keeffe became unhappy with her paintings. She decided that her work reflected other people's visions rather than her own.

Georgia O'Keeffe was a student in this 1907-8 painting class at the Art Students League of New York. The instructor, William Merritt Chase, awarded her first prize for a naturalistic still life.

Corn, Dark I, 1924. *Georgia O'Keeffe became known for her bold close-ups of flowers and plants.*

She bravely destroyed all her work and began anew with a fresh sense of style and color. When an important New York City art gallery displayed ten of her new drawings, the praise was immediate. All at once she was an important artist. She eventually married the owner of the gallery, Alfred Steiglitz, who was also a well-known photographer.

Georgia O'Keeffe began to spend long summers alone in New Mexico in 1929. She found the light, landscape, and solitude stimulating. She lived in New York City, the center of American art, during the winter. She moved permanently to Ghost Ranch in New Mexico in 1949, three years after her husband died. With each year she became more famous. She won the Medal of Freedom in 1977, and the National Medal of Arts in 1985.

Georgia O'Keeffe's style was unique. Many of her paintings feature details of large, bright flowers and objects from the desert like sun-bleached bones. She often painted the same thing over and over. Each time she had a different point of view.

Eleanor Roosevelt

Born: 1884, New York, NY
Died: 1962, New York, NY

Eleanor Roosevelt described herself as "a solemn child, without beauty . . . entirely lacking in the spontaneous joy and mirth of youth." As a grown-up, though, she ranked among the best known and most influential women in American history.

Even though Eleanor Roosevelt was born into a wealthy New York family, her childhood was unhappy. Her mother, who did not seem to love her, called her "granny" because she was so serious. When her mother, father, and one of two brothers died before she was ten, she lived with a grandmother who did not seem to love her either. A cousin described hers as "the grimmest childhood I have ever known. Who did she have? Nobody."

Eleanor Roosevelt joins California's governor at the Golden Gate Exposition in San Francisco. Her influence and non-stop pace gave new importance to the title "First Lady." (About 1939.)

At fifteen Eleanor Roosevelt was sent to a boarding school near London, England. She called her three years there the happiest of her life. The social conscience of the school's director also molded young Eleanor's character so that she dedicated her adult life to crusading for people less fortunate than herself.

She married her cousin, Franklin Delano Roosevelt, in 1905. His mother dominated the family's life. Without a real place in her own home, Eleanor Roosevelt turned outside it and found ways to be effective. She became active in the Democratic Party and also helped her husband with his political career. When

Eleanor Roosevelt traveled widely and had a genuine affection for people. It shows in this war-time meeting in New Zealand with a Maori woman. (About 1940.)

the United States entered World War I in 1917, Eleanor poured her astonishing energies into the war effort. She formed knitting circles, worked in a canteen for soldiers, and gave speeches. After the war she labored to improve the lives of working women, minorities, the poor, and the mentally ill.

Polio paralyzed Franklin Roosevelt's legs in 1921. Eleanor Roosevelt encouraged him to continue his political career and campaigned vigorously on his behalf. He was elected president of the United States in 1932, during the Great Depression. With Eleanor Roosevelt as First Lady, human rights and poverty were always kept in mind at the White House. She continued to speak widely, write articles, and soon added a regular newpaper column. She also became her husband's "legs" and made many public appearances for him.

Eleanor Roosevelt continued working even after her husband died in 1945, during his fourth term as president. That same year President Harry Truman, Franklin Roosevelt's successor, appointed her a delegate to the United Nations. She soon became the chairperson for the Commission on Human Rights, where she sponsored a Universal Declaration of Human Rights. When the declaration was passed in 1948, the General Assembly of the United Nations gave Eleanor Roosevelt a standing ovation. She didn't stop there. President Kennedy appointed her to the Commission on the Status of Women in 1961.

"You can never really live anyone else's life," she said. "The influence you exert is through your own life and what you've become yourself."

Eleanor Roosevelt helps feed the poor and out-of-work in a soup kitchen during the Great Depression in the 1930s.

A member of the Massachusetts Women's Defense Corps sends a radio message. The volunteer corps watched for airplanes and other signs of enemy activity during World War II. (Photo by Ansel Adams, 1942.)

Women in World War II

Major Charity Adams and Captain Abbie Campbell inspect the first African Americans from the Women's Army Corps (WAC) to serve overseas in World War II. They have just landed in England. Even though the WAC was racially segregated, many African-American women enlisted. They wanted to help their country, and the WAC was one of the few career opportunities open to African-American women. (1945.)

The United States entered World War II in 1941. Many men went away to fight, and the government called on women to take up the slack. Posters broadcast their importance. One poster called women "Soldiers without guns." Another told everyone "Women in the War: We Can't Win Without Them."

Women ran service clubs for soldiers, packed Red Cross parcels, sold war bonds, rationed food, and wrote letters. They also moved into the jobs that men left. They drove delivery trucks, ran farm machinery, and lay brick. They flocked to cities on the west and east coasts to take war jobs. They built airplanes, ships, ammunition, tanks, and guns. One-third of the workers in weapons' factories and forty percent in the aircraft industry were women by late 1943.

Why were women eager to fill men's shoes? For one thing women felt it was their patriotic duty. They wanted to help win the war and bring the men home as quickly as possible. Betty Kirstine Gannon answered the call for a job to help the war effort. "We went to work because of patriotism. . . . We all had somebody over there." She exchanged her job with the telephone company for one at the Naval Air Station in Seattle where she refitted seaplanes to carry wounded soldiers home.

The higher pay was also appealing. Women laboring as sales clerks and waitresses were eager for war industry jobs that paid an average of forty percent more. Katie Lee Clark Knight lived in El Paso, Texas when the war began. She moved to California at age seventeen and took a job in the shipbuilding industry. "Of course, being young, we wanted to go where the big money was," she said.

Women served in the military, too. Before the war ended, each branch of the service had a corps for women, and 350,000 women had joined. They worked as radio technicians, mechanics, typists, drivers, metalworkers, and parachute riggers. A thousand women flew airplanes in non-combat roles. More than 76,000 nurses answered the call to care for the wounded. That was almost a third of the nurses in the United States.

Women work on the tail cone assembly of an aircraft. Bandannas and "snoods," or long hairnets, were trademarks of women who made everything from bullets to bombers. (1943.)

When the war ended, war industry jobs disappeared and women lost traditionally male jobs to men returning from the war. Women were expected to return to homemaking or take less demanding jobs at lower pay. Many women left work gladly. Others felt let down. Vera-Mae Widmer Fredickson was a punch press operator when the war ended.

> The guy came back to my specific job. . . . The punch press was a man's job and had always been. . . . I went to work as a waitress. . . . Overnight, those jobs that were men's jobs vanished.

Dr. McClintock loved and valued teaching. Here she and post-graduate students investigate the molecular biology of plants. (1981.)

Barbara McClintock

Born: 1902, Hartford, CT   Died: 1992, Long Island, NY

When Barbara McClintock was eighty-one years old, she won a Nobel Prize in Medicine and Physiology. Her fame came at the end of a career filled with both successes and road blocks.

When she delivered a paper in 1951 announcing an amazing discovery about genes and chromosomes, the audience of scientists sat in silence. Even those who believed her findings ignored them. Many dismissed her results. One scientist even called her an "old bag." The research reported in that paper earned her a Nobel Prize more than thirty years later.

Barbara McClintock's parents always encouraged her to do the things that she considered important. That was not easy. She attended the College of Agriculture at Cornell at a time when women were treated with hostility there. Her intelligence and energy won her the respect of her professors, and they invited her to take graduate courses even before she had finished her undergraduate degree.

When Barbara McClintock published papers about her work in genetics at Cornell, she instantly became an internationally respected geneticist. But because she was a woman, she could not find a full-time teaching or research job at a college. For several decades Barbara McClintock took positions and fellowships that men in her field found for her. One of her students said, "She was such a tiger." She had the "stamina and brains and nerve and gall to survive" where she wasn't wanted.

Finally in 1941 she received a permanent position at Cold Springs Harbor research station on Long Island, New York. She worked there, twelve hours a day, six days a week, for the next fifty years. The National Academy of Sciences elected her a member in 1944. She served as president of the Genetic Society of America during the 1940s.

Barbara McClintock's maize or corn experiments at Cold Springs Harbor showed that chromosomes could break and come together again in a different

Throughout her whole career, Barbara McClintock used maize to conduct genetic research. (1983.)

order. Genes might sometimes be in one place on a chromosome and sometimes in another. Genes might even move from one chromosome to another.

Few scientists understood the meaning of her work at the time, but eventually her discoveries were seen as the foundation for genetic engineering. Late in her life a prominent scientist gave her the highest praise. "She was a giant figure in the history of genetics. I think she is the most important figure there is in biology in general."

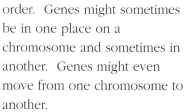

Dr. McClintock looks over a field with a colleague. She was involved in every phase of maize research from breeding to planting to harvesting. "She had a feeling for the organism," one co-worker said. (1983.)

Rosa Parks is fingerprinted in Montgomery, Alabama during the bus boycott that she had started three months earlier. (1956.)

Rosa Parks & Jo Ann

Parks—
Born: 1913, Tuskegee, AL
Robinson—
Born: 1912, Culloden, GA
Died: 1992, Huntington, NY

For good reason many Americans know that Rosa Parks was the African-American woman who refused to give up her seat on the bus to a white man in Montgomery, Alabama in 1955. Her arrest ignited the African-American boycott of the Montgomery bus system that became one of the most successful campaigns for civil rights in American history. Few people, though, have ever heard of Jo Ann Robinson or know that her leadership launched the bus boycott.

Jo Ann Robinson was the youngest of twelve children. Her father died when she was six years old, and the family moved from Culloden, Georgia to nearby Macon. She worked hard in school and became valedictorian of her high school class. She graduated from college, taught school, and married. When the couple's only child died, the marriage fell apart. Jo Ann Robinson went back to school and earned a Master's degree.

Soon she was teaching English at Alabama State College in Montgomery, Alabama. There she became active in Montgomery's Women's Political Council, a professional African-American women's group that worked for community interests. Before long she was the group's president. Many African-American women had suffered humiliating experiences on Montgomery's public buses. The Women's

Political Council decided that only a boycott of the bus system could change that. The paths of Jo Ann Robinson and Rosa Parks soon crossed to make this happen.

Rosa Parks was raised by her mother and grandparents in Pine Level, Alabama. Her mother taught in country schools and her grandparents were often ill, so young Rosa cooked and cared for the whole family. At eleven she moved to Montgomery to go to a private school and live with an aunt. She cleaned two of the classrooms to earn her school tuition. She married in 1932, and she and her husband settled in Montgomery. There in 1943 she became one of the first women members of the National Association for the Advancement of Colored People (NAACP). She served as its secretary until 1956.

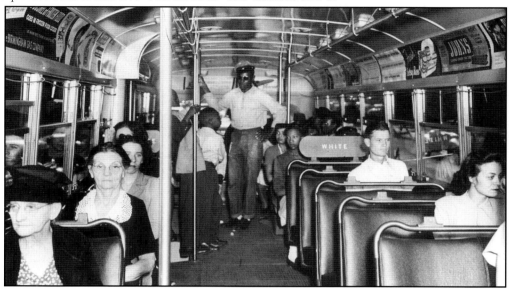

When their section of the bus was full, African Americans had to stand even if the white section had empty seats.

On December 1, 1955, Rosa Parks took the bus home from her job as a tailor at a Montgomery department store. She sat just behind the white section of the bus. When that section was full, she was asked to give up her seat to a white man. She refused. Like other women who had refused before her, Rosa Parks was arrested.

Jo Ann Robinson decided that the time was right for the one-day bus boycott that the Women's Political Council wanted. She and several students printed and distributed over fifty thousand leaflets calling for the boycott. The one-day boycott was such a success that Montgomery's African-American leaders decided to extend it. Martin Luther King, Jr. became the most prominent of these. African Americans would not ride the buses until they had the right to sit in any vacant seat. Since most of the passengers had been African Americans, both the city and the bus company lost money. More than a year later the United States Supreme Court ruled that the segregation of Montgomery's bus system was unconstitutional. African Americans could now sit in any vacant seat. The protest that Rosa Parks began and Jo Ann Robinson and the Women's Political Council seized upon became one of the greatest victories for African-American civil rights.

Jo Ann Robinson is an unsung hero of the Montgomery bus boycott and the African-American fight for civil rights.

Rachel Carson combined science and fine writing to convince the country that pesticides were damaging the Earth.

Rachel Carson

Born: 1907, Springdale, PA   Died: 1964, Silver Spring, MD

Rachel Carson's book, *Silent Spring*, showed the danger of chemicals to life on Earth and triggered the environmental movement in the United States.

Rachel Carson was a bright, quiet child who loved to read, write, and observe nature. Even when she was young, she was a talented writer. As a ten-year-old she won a story contest in a children's magazine. At Pennsylvania College for Women she first studied literature, but turned to biology after a class with an inspiring teacher.

Rachel Carson went on to study genetics at the Johns Hopkins University and biology at the Marine Biological Laboratory in Woods Hole, Massachusetts. When

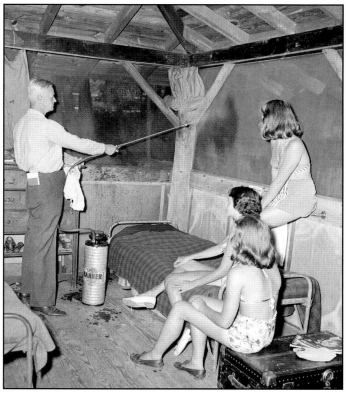

her sister died in 1936, she suddenly had two young nieces to support and needed a steady job. The United States Bureau of Fisheries hired her as one of its first women scientists. She soon published several articles and a book. Her work combined her love for biology and literature.

While working as a biologist and chief editor with the Fish and Wildlife Service, she wrote a second book. It made her famous. Called *The Sea Around Us*, it was a best seller for a year and a half and won both the National Book Award and the *New York Times* poll for the year's best book. She resigned from her job in 1951 to write full-time.

Rachel Carson wrote a third book about the seashore, but her fourth and last book had the greatest impact. Written between 1958 and 1962, *Silent Spring* opened the eyes of the public to the dangers of frequent spraying with DDT. Rachael Carson showed that birds feeding on insects and plants sprayed with DDT laid eggs with weaker shells. The result was fewer birds.

The public began to question DDT's widespread use and to ask whether other pesticides and chemicals might also harm the planet. President John Kennedy established a task force on pesticides. The movement to protect the environment was born.

When the book appeared, many people tried to discredit Rachel Carson. Others laughed at her fears. Even so, she knew that she had to tell the truth, no matter what. "There would be no peace for me if I kept silent." Decades after her death, her voice is still strong.

Rachael Carson died two years after Silent Spring *was* published. During those years she spoke to many groups. "To save the planet," she said, "it is necessary to prove . . . our mastery, not of nature, but of ourselves."

Dolores Huerta is a dynamic speaker. Cesar Chavez, founder of the United Farm Workers, called her "totally fearless, both mentally and physically." (About 1980.)

Dolores Huerta

Born: 1930, Dawson, NM

Dolores Huerta, a leader and co-founder of the United Farm Workers Union and the mother of eleven children, is one of the most effective and well-known labor activists of this century.

When Dolores Huerta was very young, she moved with her mother and two brothers to Stockton, California. While a grandfather cared for the children, her mother supported the family by working as a waitress during the day and in a cannery at night. Eventually the family bought a boarding house that Dolores and her brothers helped run. She went to college to earn a teaching certificate, but became discouraged with teaching because the children of farm workers came to school needing food and clothing more than they needed knowledge.

Dolores Huerta found a new path for her life and a way to help farm workers in the mid-1950s. She joined the Community Service Organization (CSO), a Hispanic self-help association. She was energetic, bold, outspoken, and effective, and she soon held important positions in the CSO despite her youth and gender. As a CSO member she organized farm laborers, registered them to vote, and worked for improvements in Hispanic neighborhoods. She was the chief lobbyist for the CSO at the California state capital in 1959. Her efforts were important. She

helped persuade California lawmakers to grant social security and welfare benefits to farm laborers.

Dolores Huerta became convinced that raising the wages of farm workers was the best way to improve their lives. So she left the CSO in 1962 and moved to Delano, California. There she helped Cesar Chavez start a union for farm laborers that was eventually called the United Farm Workers Union. She quickly became the union's chief negotiator and sat across the table from fruit and vegetable growers, drawing up contracts that guaranteed decent pay and housing for farm laborers. She was also a coordinator during the grape, lettuce, and wine boycotts that forced California growers to negotiate with the farm workers.

Her life as a union organizer was not always peaceful. She was arrested more than twenty-two times, and police broke six of her ribs and ruptured her spleen during a demonstration in 1988. After months of recovery Dolores Huerta renewed her struggle to win better lives for Hispanics and farm workers.

A child works in an onion field in 1978. Even today many children pick crops instead of going to school. Dolores Huerta knew that the best way to end child labor was to pay grownups higher wages. (Mettler, California, 1978.)

Dolores Huerta, on the right, talks to grape workers during the 1960s. She traveled up and down California, bringing workers into a new farm union. (1976.)

111

Betty Friedan put into words the discontent that many American women felt. She was still a major force in the women's movement decades after The Feminine Mystique *was published.*

Betty Friedan

Born: 1921, Peoria, IL

Betty Friedan's book, *The Feminine Mystique*, launched a new struggle for equality by American women. When Betty Friedan was young, her mother told her not to abandon her dreams. Her mother had left a job on a newspaper when she married and was never content with her life as a housewife. She wanted her daughter's life to be different.

For years young Betty followed her mother's advice. She wrote for the school newspaper and started a literary journal in high school. She graduated from Smith College with highest honors in 1942. The reward for her hard work was a graduate fellowship studying with one of the most famous psychologists in the world. Betty Friedan was not sure she wanted to be a psychologist, so after a year she gave up the fellowship and took a job in New York City as a journalist.

Soon her life changed even more. She married and moved to the suburbs near New York City. She worked on a newspaper and had a child. When she told her boss that she was pregnant with a second child, he fired her. Her boss made it clear that she could have a career or a family but not both.

Even though Betty Friedan wrote magazine articles at home, she felt trapped, just like her mother had years before. Most studies about women published after World War II said that women who took care of husbands, children, and houses should feel fulfilled. Betty Friedan knew that she did not feel satisfied, and she wondered if other women did.

Most young women today use computers and word-processing programs instead of manual typewriters like the one Betty Friedan used when she was young. Even so, their opportunity for higher education and jobs is linked to the movement Betty Freidan helped ignite.

Betty Friedan began studying women and their place in society. She sent a questionnaire to former classmates from college. Many replied that they were unhappy housewives. Betty Friedan became convinced that women wanted and needed careers outside the home to be happy. She published *The Feminine Mystique* about her findings. Millions of women read the book. It put into words their desire to have both families and careers.

Betty Friedan plays with her daughter Emily, one of her three children. In 1963 she published a book saying that women needed careers as well as motherhood to be happy.

The Feminine Mystique was only part of Betty Friedan's work for women. She and others founded the National Organization of Women (NOW) in 1966, and she served as the organization's first president. NOW worked for the right of women to compete for any job and receive the same pay as men.

Betty Friedan has written and edited other books about women's issues, but her first one, *The Feminine Mystique*, started a revolution to change women's place in society that continues today.

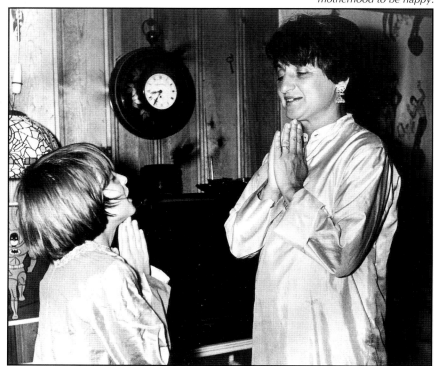

Toni Morrison talks about writing plays with a college class in 1985.

Toni Morrison

Born: 1931, Loraine, OH

Toni Morrison, winner of the 1993 Nobel Prize for Literature, is among the most important writers in the United States. She is also a powerful voice for African Americans and women.

Toni Morrison was born Chloe Anthony Wofford and in high school changed her name to Toni. She was the granddaughter of southern sharecroppers who moved north to find education and opportunity for their children. Storytelling in the African-American tradition and pride in black ability filled her childhood. When her father welded a perfect seam for a ship, he put his name nearby to show his pride in his work.

Toni Morrison could already read when she started school, and she read broadly as a teenager. When she graduated from high school with honors, she surprised her parents by going to college instead of looking for a job and marrying. She earned a degree in English from Howard University in Washington, D.C. in 1953, and two years later received a graduate degree from Cornell University.

Toni Morrison was teaching literature and writing in several colleges when her marriage of seven years ended in divorce in 1964. To support her two sons, she

> ## "Had I lived the life that the state planned for me from the beginning, I would have lived and died in somebody else's kitchen, on somebody else's land, and never written a word. That knowledge is bone deep, and it informs everything I do." (Speech, 1986)

took a job in publishing and was soon a senior editor at Random House where she made it a point to encourage African-American writers.

Toni Morrison began to write in the late 1950s. In 1970 she published her first novel, *The Bluest Eye*, based on a childhood memory of a black girl who had prayed for blue eyes. Even in her first book, Toni Morrison's insights into the minds of her characters drew readers into their lives.

> Adults do not talk to us—they give directions. They issue orders without providing information. . . . When we catch colds, they shake their heads in disgust at our lack of consideration. How, they ask, do you expect anybody to get anything done if you all are sick?

Song of Solomon and *Tar Baby*, her third and fourth novels, established her as a major American writer. For her haunting fifth novel *Beloved*, in 1987, Toni Morrison won the distinguished Pulitzer Prize. She has since added *Jazz* and *Paradise* to her list of novels. Toni Morrison became a professor at Princeton University in 1989. She continues to write both fiction and non-fiction, focusing on African-American history, women, society, and literature. She was the first African-American to win a Nobel Prize for Literature.

Toni Morrison's novels use words artistically, tell gripping stories, and ask moral questions. They also say something to women about their past. (1999.)

Sandra Day O'Connor

Born: 1930, El Paso, TX

In 1981 Sandra Day O'Connor became the first woman justice of the United States Supreme Court.

Growing up on the Lazy B, a large ranch in southeastern Arizona, young Sandra learned to be self-reliant. By age ten she could drive a tractor and a car. "We played with dolls, but we knew what to do with screwdrivers and nails." Since there were no schools near the ranch, she and her sister lived much of the year with their grandmother, across the state line in El Paso, Texas.

At sixteen she set out for Stanford University. Four years later she graduated with high honors. Next came three distinguished years at Stanford's law school, but when she finished in 1952, she had a hard time finding a job as a lawyer because she was a woman. A major law firm in Los Angeles offered her a job—as a secretary. She finally became a deputy county attorney in San Mateo, California.

Sandra Day O'Connor soon moved to Frankfurt, Germany with her new husband and worked as a civilian lawyer for the United States Army there. Later the young family settled in Phoenix, Arizona, and for five years she raised her three sons and did not work outside the home. When she took up her career again, one record-breaking achievement followed another.

She became an Assistant Attorney General of Arizona in 1965. She entered politics and was elected to the Arizona State Senate as a Republican in 1969. When she became the majority leader of the State Senate three years later, she was the first woman in the country to be a majority leader of a state senate. She was elected a judge of the Maricopa County Superior Court in 1974 and then became a judge of the Arizona Court of Appeals.

Sandra Day O'Connor stands with the other Supreme Court judges in 1981 when she became the first women on the court. Ruth Bader Ginsburg became the second twelve years later.

President Ronald Reagan nominated her to the United States Supreme Court in 1981. Confirmed by the Senate in a vote of 99 to 0, Sandra Day O'Connor became the first woman in history to sit on the United States Supreme Court.

May Lin poses in 1981 with a model of the Vietnam Veterans Memorial, the most famous monument she has yet designed.

Maya Lin

Born: 1959, Athens, Ohio

Imagine becoming famous at twenty-one. It happened to Maya Lin. During her final year as a student at Yale University, she entered a competition to design the Vietnam Veterans Memorial in Washington, D.C. Her proposal was chosen over 1420 other entries. In the years since, she has designed other monuments and become even more famous.

About 25,000,000 people have visited the Vietnam Veterans Memorial since 1982. That makes it one of the most popular sights in Washington, D.C. (1982.)

Maya Lin was born into a talented and successful family. After her parents fled from China in the 1940s, her mother became a professor of Asian literature at Ohio University. Her father, a ceramist, became dean of the school of fine arts at Ohio State University.

Maya Lin was always gifted and independent. She was a strong student who spent a lot of time alone. She hiked, read, and worked with clay, bronze, and other materials in her father's studio. She took some college-level courses in high school and also worked part-time at a McDonald's restaurant. A high school course about death fascinated Maya Lin. In college she studied architecture. During her free time she visited cemeteries and photographed headstones. She merged her interests in cemeteries and architecture when she designed the Vietnam Veterans Memorial.

Winning the competition for the memorial did not make Maya Lin popular with everyone. Some people doubted that the best idea could come from a young woman. Some did not like the way the memorial looked. Others were angry that an Asian American was designing the memorial for a war the United States had fought in Asia. Hostility toward Maya Lin was so great among former soldiers that she was not even mentioned when the monument was dedicated in 1982.

More than a million people a year visit the two black granite tablets set in the side of a small hill in Washington, D.C. Many touch some of the 58,000 names of United States soldiers killed during the war. Maya Lin's monument has become a site of healing for those who lost friends and family in the war.

Rosa Parks, in the center, visits the Civil Rights Memorial in Montgomery, Alabama, another monument that Maya Lin designed.

Maya Lin also designed the Civil Rights Memorial in Montgomery, Alabama. The names and dates of forty racial murders are carved on a round slab of black granite with water flowing slowly over it. Like Maya Lin's other designs, the Civil Rights Memorial helps people appreciate the sacrifices others have made.

Jackie Joyner-Kersee

Born: 1962, East St. Louis, IL

Jackie Joyner-Kersee waves a bouquet during the 1988 Olympic Games in Seoul after setting a new world record as the heptathlon gold medalist.

When Jackie Joyner was born, her grandmother insisted that she be named after First Lady Jacqueline Kennedy, the wife of President John Kennedy. "Someday this girl will be first lady of something," her grandmother said. She was right. Jackie Joyner-Kersee overcame a poverty-stricken childhood to become one of the greatest athletes in the world.

The second child of teenage parents, Jackie Joyner was born and grew up in a run-down and sometimes violent neighborhood. At eleven she saw a man shot down in the street. Because her mother had her first baby at sixteen, she did not allow young Jackie to date until she was eighteen. Instead, her mother encouraged her daughter to study hard and succeed in spite of her surroundings. Joyner concentrated on her studies and sports and became outstanding at both.

Jackie Joyner-Kersee began entering track meets as a nine-year-old and quickly began capturing first-place trophies. At fourteen she was national junior champion of the Pentathlon, a track and field competition with five events. She also set records in the long jump, led her school to victory in basketball, and kept her grades high.

Joyner started college at UCLA in 1980 with the help of a basketball scholarship. There she worked with coach Bob Kersee, whom she married after she finished college. He encouraged her to train for the heptathlon, a new event with seven track and field sports.

Jackie Joyner-Kersee was soon a heptathlon star. At the 1984 Olympic games she won a silver medal in the event. She scored an amazing 7,291 points in the

Jackie Joyner-Kersee sails over a hurdle in a 100 meter heptathlon heat in Seoul, Korea during the Olympic Games. Girls' sports received a real boost in 1972. Title IX of the Educational Amendments Act said that public school sports for girls must have the same funding as sports for boys. As a result the number of girls participating in sports has jumped from 290,000 to 2,200,00 in tirty years.

heptathlon at the Goodwill Games in Moscow two years later. That same year she was given the Sullivan Award and named America's most outstanding amateur athlete of the year.

More astounding victories followed. In the 1988 Olympic Games, Jackie Joyner-Kersee won a gold medal for the heptathlon. Four years later at age thirty, she again took home an Olympic gold medal for the event. She was the first woman to win consecutive medals in the heptathlon. Her outstanding feats have made her one of the greatest athletes in history.

Heather Rosenman works full time as a graphic designer. Like millions of American women she also picks up the children from day care, shops for groceries, and takes care of the house.

Superwomen

At the end of the twentieth century, American women could make more choices about their lives than ever before. Since more than half the women with school-age children worked outside the home, new family patterns were developing. Many couples shared housework. Some took turns preparing meals and caring for children. More jobs for women meant that more women could support themselves. Many decided to stay single, and fewer men and women stayed in unhappy marriages.

Many American women tried to be superwomen. They stepped into jobs that were open to women for the first time in history. Balancing jobs and families was harder than many had expected. They tried to give one hundred percent to both family and job. Some felt let down when that was impossible.

Diane Sears was a lawyer with a large firm as the century ended. She and her husband hired a housekeeper to care for their two children so that they could spend long days at their offices. Her husband often cooked on the weekends or the family ate fast food. Sears had a successful career, but she worried about decent day care and not spending enough time with her children.

Despite the changes in the way families operated, women with busy working lives still shouldered more responsibility than men for children and the home.

Most working women spent eight times longer on household duties and child care than men. When hours worked outside and inside the home were added together, women on average worked 780 hours a year longer than most men. That was three extra months of eight hour days every year.

Some American women faced poverty and other obstacles. Adela Mendez met tough challenges and came out on top. Born in a small village in El Salvador, she became pregnant at seventeen and dropped out of school. El Salvador was caught in a civil war, and her young son's father did not want to join either the army or the guerrillas. He fled to the United States. Adela Mendez soon followed. She knew it would be a difficult and dangerous trip, so she left her son with her parents.

She flew to Mexico City and made her way north. At Tijuana she crossed the border in the trunk of a car with several other people she didn't know. She was lucky. She made it to Los Angeles where her husband was waiting.

She took a job cleaning houses and had two more children. She works five or six days a week cleaning houses while her husband does construction work. She has an

Adela Mendez and her daughters Joanna and Jessica focus on Joanna's homework. Jessica, a sixth-grader, serves as the English translator for the family.

employment card that allows her to work in the United States and is working toward citizenship. At night she takes English lessons. Like many American moms, she helps her children with their homework.

Going back to El Salvador would be dangerous for Adela Mendez. Her father was killed in the war after she came to the United States, and her fifteen-year-old brother was kidnapped by guerrillas and has disappeared. When the son she had left in El Salvador was eighteen, he made the same difficult journey she had made eleven years earlier and joined the rest of the family in Los Angeles.

Many young women now study advanced physics in high school. (1998.)

Frustrated with an office job, Lt. Mary Louise Jorgensen joined the Navy in 1972 and became a tactical jet pilot. She was the second woman in the navy to qualify to fly a jet. (1977.)

Conclusion

America's past is filled with remarkable women who acted with vision, resolve, and energy. In spite of the burdens and responsibilities they shouldered, earlier generations called them inferior and bridled them with restrictions. Most women could not own property, control their own money, attend secondary school or college, hold most jobs, seek political office, or even speak in public. Most women who worked could earn only low pay.

Through the centuries American women have knocked down barriers. They have expanded their world and changed perceptions about themselves. Many now hold jobs that pay enough to support themselves and their children. They speak out, and they lead. American women sit on the Supreme Court, serve as ambassadors to other countries, drive trucks, run large businesses, and attended universities and teach in them. They participate in countless other arenas once closed to them.

No one knows what awaits America's girls when they become the women of the twenty-first century. Old barriers will fall away, and new challenges will arise. Some of tomorrow's women will focus on supporting themselves and their families. Others will make new discoveries or enter fields still closed to women today. No matter what they do, centuries of America's daughters have left strong legacies to inspire them.

Miss Hanson binds grain near Milton, North Dakota during the early 1900s. Women have always helped run family farms, doing whatever needed to be done. (About 1905.)

Want to Know More?

Many publishers have individual books or series about American women. Check your school, bookstore, and library for those available in your area. You can also use Amazon.com or other online bookstores to search for titles by subject or person. Here are a few good references.

For heavy-duty insight and reference about women during different times in American history, see the eleven volume *Young Oxford History of American Women* published by Oxford University Press.

The kid version of *Women's Firsts: Milestones in Women's History* from Gale Research is another good reference.

For information about famous women from all over the world, try *Herstory: Women Who Changed the World* from Viking Children's Books.

Practically all women sewed in the 1800s and their quilts were extraordinary records of their lives. Women sewed quilts honoring a marriage or the birth of a baby. They sewed scenes of everyday life and quilts with political messages. Friends put together album quilts so that departing pioneers would remember them. Quilting was creative, practical and social. Here quiltmakers, friends and relations gather sometime between 1890 and 1910.

The Scholastic Encyclopedia of Women in the United States has short biographies of two hundred famous American women.

There are also hundreds of exciting resources about American women available to any school, library, or child with access to the Internet. Here are a few of them.

The Premier Search Directory for Women Online leads to a huge list of varied web sites. http://wwwomen.com!

Gale Research has a free site with biographies, quizzes, timelines, and more. http://www.gale.com/gale/cwh/cwhset.html

Britannica Online's *Women in American History* is rich with biographies, multi-media resources, and links to other sites. Sometimes it is free. http://women.eb.com/women

The National Women's History Project site features ideas for projects that kids, teachers, librarians, and parents can use. It also has a catalogue for ordering books and other materials about women's history. http://www.nwhp.org/

The National Women's Hall of Fame site features great women of the past and present. http://www.greatwomen.org/index.html

The United States Census Bureau has statistics on almost anything. You may have to search awhile, and if you want a lot of data you may have to download a special program so that your computer can read it. http://www.census.gov/

The Museum of Afro American History web site has several powerful recordings of women and men telling about their lives as slaves. http://www.afroammuseum.org/

Find written accounts of women who were once slaves on-line from *Duke University*. http://scriptorium.lib.duke.edu/collections/african-american-women.html

The site *Women of the West* tells the stories of a few women who went west. http://www.over-land.com/westpers2.html

Women Who Have Made History features interesting and important women who are not well known. http://www.geocities.com/Wellesley/3059/history.html

For more about witches see *Witchcraft in Salem Village*. http://etext.virginia.edu/salem/witchcraft/

The National Archives Just for Kids page from the Hoover Library has changing resources. A recent adventure was a trip along the trail Laura Ingalls's family took as pioneers. http://hoover.nara.gov/kids/index.html

Find out more about women Nobel Prize winners on the *Nobel Prize Internet Archive*. http://www.almaz.com/nobel/women.html

A Celebration of Women Writers leads to biographies and other information about hundreds of women writers. http://www.cs.cmu.edu/afs/cs.cmu.edu/user/mmbt/www/women/celebration.html.

What did you do in the war, Grandma? shares the personal stories of more than two dozen women during World War II. The site was compiled by high school students and has tips on how to use oral history in teaching. http://www.stg.brown.edu/projects/WWII_Women/tocCS.html

Acknowledgements

Grateful acknowledgment is made to the following for permission to reprint previously published material:

Excerpt from *Root of Bitterness: Documents of the Social History of American Women*, second edition, edited by Nancy Cott et al., © 1996. Reprinted by permission of Northeastern University Press.

Excerpt from *Yankee Women: Gender Battles in the Civil War* by Elizabeth D. Leonard, © 1994. Reprinted by permission of W.W. Norton & Company, Inc.

Excerpt from *A Midwife's Tale: The Life of Martha Ballard Based on her Diary, 1785-1812* by Laurel Thatcher Ulrich, © 1990. Reprinted by permission of Random House, Inc.

Excerpts from *A Mouthful of Rivets* by Nancy Baker Wise and Christy Wise, © 1994. Reprinted by permission of Jossey-Bass, Inc.

Excepts from *The Bluest Eye* by Toni Morrison, © 1970. Reprinted by permission of Alfred A. Knopf, Inc.

The author extends her gratitude to all those at Bates College who assisted with this book. Warmest thanks also go to Betsy Hanscom, Joan Macri, Susan Allison, Carolyn Crocker, publisher and photo-researcher Linda Pillsbury, and above all to Michael and Austin.

Picture Credits

We thank the following for their help and for the use of the pictures: **Cover**, UPI/Corbis-Bettmann ©; **iii**, Courtesy, Colorado Historical Society, #F28537; **iv**, McLeod Family; **v-vi**, Fred Hulstrand History in Pictures Collection, NDIRS-NDSU, Fargo,ND; **1**, Joe Pineiro, Columbia University; **3**, Fine Arts Museums of San Francisco, Gift of Mr. and Mrs. John D. Rockefeller 3rd, 1979.7.3; **4**, Library of Congress, LC-USZ62-49632; **5**, Picture Collection, The Branch Libraries, The New York Public Library; **7**, Library of Congress, LC-USZ62-069999; **8**, Library of Congress, LC-USZ62-60814; **9**, Library of Congress, LC-USZ62-56416; **10**, Library of Congress, LC-USZ62-873; **11**, Library of Congress, LC-USZ62-1495; **12**, Library of Congress, LC-USZ62-49744; **13** (top) Library of Congress, LC-USZ62-49744, (bottom) Library of Congress, LC-USA7-24315; **14**, Library of Congress, PS-712-C25RBD; **15**, National Archives, 208-LU-25-J-5; **16**, Library of Congress, LC-USZ62-2287; **17**, Museum of the City of New York, The J. Clarence Davies Scrapbook; **19**, Library of Congress, LC-USZ62-078099; **20-21**, Library of Congress, LC-711708-262-33994; **21**, Library of Congress, LC-USZ262-15384; **22**, The Schlesinger Library, Radcliffe College; **23**, Library of Congress, LC-USZ62-31953; **24**, Library of Congress, LC-USZ62-20966; **25**, (top) Library of Congress, LC-USZ62-51641, (bottom) Library of Congress, LC-USZ62-476; **26-27**, Library of Congress, LC-USZ62-046287; **28**, (top) Library of Congress, LC-USZ62-55354, (bottom) Library of Congress, LC-USZ62-3239; **29**, The Historical Society of York county, PA, Lewis Miller (1796-1882); **30**, Library of Congress, LC-USZ62-24492; **31**, (top) Litchfield Historical Society, by Robert Houser, (bottom) The Historical Society of York county, PA, Lewis Miller (1796-1882); **32-33**, Duke University, Rare Book, Manuscript, & Special Collections Library; **34**, Gift of Joseph W.R. Rogers and Mary C. Rogers, Courtesy, Museum of Fine Arts, Boston, E10844; **35**, The Connecticut Historical Society, Hartford, Connecticut; **36**, Courtesy, American Antiquarian Society; **37**, (top) Courtesy of the Society for the Preservation of New England Antiquities, (bottom) Library of Congress, LC-USZ62-29058; **38**, Maryland Historical Society, Baltimore, Maryland; **39**, (top) Library of Congress, LC-USZ62-10474, (bottom) Library of Congress, LC-USZ62-12532; **40**, Library of Congress, LC-USZ62-56850; **41**, Library of Congress, LC-USZ62-31876; **42**, Bequest of Winslow Warren, Courtesy, Museum of Fine Arts, Boston; **43**, Courtesy, Winterthur Museum; **44**, National Life Insurance Company, Montpelier, VT; **45**, Library of Congress, LCUSZ62-704; **46**, Library of Congress, LC-USZ62-202; **47**, Library of Congress, LC-USZ62-17627; **48**, Weathersfield Historical Society; **49**, (top) Wellcome Institute Library, London, Ref: V0014923B00, (bottom) Library of Congress, LC-USZ62-39444; **50-51**, Nebraska State Historical Society, Collection No. RG2608, Photographer S.D. Butcher; **52**, Library of Congress, LC-USZ62-2672; **53**, Courtesy, Colorado Historical Society, #F-28412; **54**, Library of Congress, LC-USZ6-353; **55**, Library of Congress, LC-USZ62-32049; **56**, Library of Congress, LC-USZ62-43346; **57**, Library of Congress, LC-USZ62-5292; **58**, Photo by Ben Wittick, Courtesy Museum of New Mexico, Neg. No. 3083; **59**, Library of Congress, LC-USZ62-40500; **60-61**, Emma Willard School Archives; **62-63**, Special Collections, Vassar College Libraries, Poughkeepsie, NY; **64**, UPI/Corbis-Bettman ©; **65**, (top) Library of Congress, LC 711708 262-75975, (bottom) Photographs and Prints Division, Schomburg Center for Research in Black Culture, The New York Public Library, Astor, Lenox and Tilden Foundations; **66, 67** (top) The Schlesinger Library, Radcliffe College; (bottom) Library of Congress, LC 711708 262-41838; **68**, Moorland-Spingarn Research Center, Howard University; **69**, Photographs and Prints Division, Schomburg Center for Research in Black Culture, The New York Public Library, Astor, Lenox and Tilden Foundations; **70**, Massachusetts Commandery Military Order of the Loyal Legion and the US Army Military History Institute, Carlisle, PA; **71**, Courtesy of the Trustees of Boston Public Library; **72**, Collection of The New-York Historical Society, #48099; **73**, Chicago Historical Society, #ICHi-22103; **74**, The Schlesinger Library, Radcliffe College; **75**, Library of Congress, LC-USZ62-2053; **76**, Library of Congress, LC 800689 USZ61-791; **77**, UPI/Corbis-Bettman ©; **78**, Library of Congress, LC BH1834-55-711706; **79**, Library of Congress; **80**, Nevada Historical Society; **81**, (top) Library of Congress, LC 902076-LCUS262-17618, (bottom) Photo by John K. Hillers, Courtesy New Mexico, Neg. No. 102081; **82**, Photo by Ben Wittick, Courtesy Museum of New Mexico, Neg. No. 16068; **83**, (top) Photo by Ben Wittick, Courtesy Museum of New Mexico, Neg. No. 15475, (bottom) National Anthropological Archives, Smithsonian Institution; **84-85**, Courtesy of Wellesley College, Photo by John Mottern; **86**, Library of Congress, LC800691-262-43683; **87**, (top) Linda Goodman Pillsbury, (bottom) Kansas State Historical Society; **88**, Library of Congress, LC 800689-USZ62-7089; **89**, (top) Corbis/Genevieve Naylor ©, (bottom) Library of Congress, LC 711705-LC-U9-23116-21; **90**, Library of Congress, LC 813510-USZ62-051199; **91**, (top) Sharlot Hall Museum, Prescott, Arizona, (bottom) Library of Congress, LC 813510-USZ62-086177; **92**, Baldwin H. Ward/Corbis-Bettman ©; **93**, (top) Robert F. Wagner Labor Archives, New York University, Rose Schneiderman Collection, (bottom) National Archives; **94**, Photo by Wyatt Davis, Courtesy Museum of New Mexico, Neg. No. 44191; **95**, (top) Photo by Tyler Dingee, Courtesy Museum of New Mexico, Neg. No. 73453, (bottom) Photo by Tyler Dingee, Courtesy Museum of New Mexico, Neg. No. 120169; **96**, The Schlesinger Library, Radcliffe College; **97**, (top) National Archives, (bottom) The Schlesinger Library, Radcliffe College; **98**, (top) Courtesy Museum of New Mexico, Neg. No. 9763, (bottom) Art Students League of New York; **99**, The Metroplitan Museum of Art, The Alfred Stieglitz Collection, 1949. (50.236.1) © 1999 The Georgia O'Keeffe Foundation/Artists Rights Society (ARS), New York; **100**, Library of Congress, LC USZ62-047999; **101**, (top) Library of Congress LC USZ62-064437, (bottom) National Archives; **102**, (top) The Schlesinger Library, Radcliffe College, (bottom) National Archives; **103**, National Archives; **104-105**, Cold Spring Harbor Laboratory Archives; **106**, AP/Wide World Photos; **107**, (top) Birmingham Public Library Archives, Catalog #49.59, (bottom) Booker T. Lee; **108**, Underwood & Underwood/Corbis-Bettmann ©; **109**, (top) Corbis/Bettmann ©, (bottom) Library of Congress, LC US262-107991; **110-111**, Archives of Labor and Urban Affairs, Wayne State University; **112-113**, The Schlesinger Library, Radcliffe College; **114**, Corbis/Bettmann ©; **115**, Linda Goodman Pillsbury; **116-117**, Courtesy Ronald Reagan Library; **118**, (top) UPI/Corbis-Bettmann ©, (bottom) National Park Service, courtesy of www.parkphotos.com; **119**, Alabama Bureau of Tourism & Travel; **120**, Reuters/Corbis-Bettmann ©; **121**, Reuters/Corbis-Bettmann ©; **122-123**, Linda Goodman Pillsbury; **124**, (top) Leah H. Pillsbury, (bottom) Corbis-Bettmann ©; **125**, Fred Hulstrand History in Pictures Collection, NDIRS-NDSU, Fargo, ND; **126**, Glendora Hutson Collection, Courtesy of Hearts and Hands Media Arts; **129**, Fred Hulstrand History in Pictures Collection, NDIRS-NDSU, Fargo, ND; **130**, Linda Goodman Pillsbury; **Back cover**, Courtesy Museum of New Mexico, Neg. No. 15069

Index

Mrs. Mary F. Bannerman, on the right, waits on customers as they try on hats in her millinery shop in Park Rover, North Dakota. (1910-1919.)

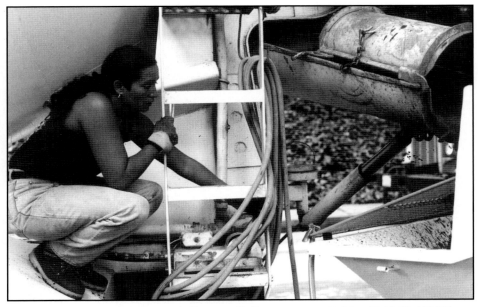

Amelia Salcido drives and operates a cement mixer. "I keep telling my friends they should try this job. It pays a lot more than waitressing and is a lot more fun." (1999)